Promoting Cultural Sensitivity in Supervision

Promoting Cultural Sensitivity in Supervision: A Manual for Practitioners provides a roadmap for practicing and experienced supervisors to promote and integrate cultural sensitivity into the core of their work. This book is organized into four seamless, interrelated sections that are essential to developing a Multicultural Relational Perspective (MRP) in supervision: conceptual, structural, strategies and techniques, and evaluation tools. The **Conceptual** section provides an overview of the theory that underpins an MRP, and the **Structural** section provides the reader with two specific strategies for concretizing the conceptual framework. The **Strategies and Techniques** section includes a variety of chapters that provide supervisors and supervisees with hands-on tools for navigating difficult diversity-related conversations in supervision and beyond, as well as an array of exercises that supervisors can employ to enhance cultural sensitivity. The **Evaluation Tools** section provides sample instruments that can be implemented to evaluate the objectives of the entire supervisory process. For the convenience of readers, additional photocopiable supervisory resources have also been included at the end of the manual. This manual is intended for supervisors, trainers, clinicians, and trainees.

Kenneth V. Hardy, PhD, is a professor at Drexel University in Philadelphia, Pennsylvania, director of the Eikenberg Institute for Relationships in New York, New York, and is also the founder of the Eikenberg Academy for Social Justice. He is the former director of clinical training and research at Syracuse University in New York as well as the former director of The Center for Children, Families, and Trauma at the Ackerman Institute for the Family in New York, New York. Dr. Hardy has had extensive experience training and supervising both beginning and seasoned therapists working in a variety of clinical settings.

Toby Bobes, PhD, is a licensed marriage and family therapist with experience in teaching graduate-level courses for 25 years and doing clinical supervision for 18 years. She currently teaches at Pacifica Graduate Institute and formerly taught at Antioch University. Her career includes 28 years in private practice. Dr. Bobes has taught many supervision courses for the California Division of the American Association for Marriage and Family Therapy (AAMFT), and she is an AAMFT Approved Supervisor and a California Association of Marriage and Family Therapists (CAMFT) Certified Supervisor.

"Hardy and Bobes brilliantly demonstrate a much-needed specialized roadmap to understanding and integrating cultural sensitivity in clinical supervision. This manual provides practical steps to work effectively with a broad range of diverse populations. Readers will surely be challenged to reflect critically about their respective clinical inclinations and lived experiences in the area of inclusion and therapeutic practice."

Kiran S. K. Arora, PhD,
Associate Professor, Department of Counseling
and School Psychology,
Long Island University, Brooklyn

"*Promoting Cultural Sensitivity in Supervision* positions the supervisory relationship squarely in the 21st century, where privilege, oppression, and invisibility persist, and where increased multicultural visibility and consideration do not necessarily lead to greater sensitivity, even in supervision. Drs. Hardy and Bobes do not challenge the basic tenets of the supervisory relationship, so much as situate them in their historical context and, by doing so, address a long-standing need in the field for a structured, operationalized framework for applying a contextual lens to the supervisory relationship."

Christian Jordal, PhD,
Editor, *Journal of Family Psychotherapy*,
Program Director, Master of Family Therapy program,
Drexel University

Promoting Cultural Sensitivity in Supervision

A Manual for Practitioners

Edited by
Kenneth V. Hardy
and Toby Bobes

Routledge
Taylor & Francis Group

NEW YORK AND LONDON

First edition published 2017
by Routledge
711 Third Avenue, New York, NY 10017

and by Routledge
2 Park Square, Milton Park, Abingdon, Oxon, OX14 4RN

Routledge is an imprint of the Taylor & Francis Group, an informa business

Library of Congress Cataloging-in-Publication Data
Names: Hardy, Kenneth V., editor. | Bobes, Toby, 1940– editor.
Title: Promoting cultural sensitivity in supervision : a manual for practitioners /
edited by Kenneth V. Hardy, PhD and Toby Bobes, PhD.
Description: First Edition. | New York : Routledge, 2017. | Includes bibliographical
references and index.
Identifiers: LCCN 2016052992| ISBN 9780415787673 (hardcover : alk. paper) |
ISBN 9780415787680 (pbk. : alk. paper) | ISBN 9781315225791 (e-book)
Subjects: LCSH: Cross-cultural counseling. | Counseling—Study and teaching. |
Multiculturalism.
Classification: LCC BF636.7.C76 P76 2017 | DDC 658.3/02—dc23
LC record available at https://lccn.loc.gov/2016052992

ISBN: 978-0-415-78767-3 (hbk)
ISBN: 978-0-415-78768-0 (pbk)
ISBN: 978-1-315-22579-1 (ebk)

Typeset in Arial
by Florence Production Ltd, Stoodleigh, Devon, UK

Contents

List of Figures   vii
Preface   ix
Acknowledgments   xi

Part I: Conceptual Considerations   1

1   Core Supervisor Competencies   3
    Kenneth V. Hardy, PhD and Toby Bobes, PhD

2   A Developmental Model of Personal and Professional Growth   15
    Toby Bobes, PhD

3   Race Through a Trauma Lens   21
    Kenneth V. Hardy, PhD

4   "Naming It and Claiming It"—Embracing Your Identity as an Activist
    (Supervisor, Educator, Therapist)   25
    Kenneth V. Hardy, PhD

Part II: Structural Considerations   29

5   Establishing an Effective Supervisory Relationship: A Two-Step
    Process   31
    Kenneth V. Hardy, PhD and Toby Bobes, PhD

Part III: Strategies and Techniques   45

6   The Validate, Challenge, and Request Approach: A Practical Tool
    for Facilitating Difficult Dialogues   47
    Kenneth V. Hardy, PhD

7   Essential Skills for Mastering Context Talk in Supervision   55
    Kenneth V. Hardy, PhD

8   The Cultural Genogram: Key to Training Culturally Competent
    Family Therapists   61
    Kenneth V. Hardy, PhD and Tracey A. Laszloffy, PhD

9   Collaborative Training Tools for Supervisors and Supervisees   75
    Nancy Steiny, PhD

10 Promoting Cultural Sensitivity in Online and Electronically-
    Based Supervision   85
    Kenneth V. Hardy, PhD

11 Experiential Exercises   99
    Kenneth V. Hardy, PhD and Toby Bobes, PhD

Part IV: Evaluation Tools   **117**

12 The Multicultural Relational Perspective: Supervision Outcome
    Tools for Mental Health Professionals   119
    Kenneth V. Hardy, PhD

Handouts and Resources   **133**

Relational Ethics   135

Sample Case Presentation Format Using a Multicultural
Relational Perspective   137

Sample Framework for Establishing an Explicit Supervision Contract   139

Promoting Cultural Sensitivity Starter Kit   141

Professional Organizations   151

Index   153

Figures

1.1 A Context Map   10
1.2 A Context Map with Increasing Complexity   11
1.3 A Context Map with Multidirectionality   12
8.1 The Cultural Genogram   63

Preface

The rapidly changing demographics of our society make it virtually mandatory for supervisors and clinicians to develop effective strategies for attending to issues of diversity throughout all domains of the clinical process. Even when the desire and commitment to be more culturally attuned are clear, possessing the "know how" to achieve such a lofty and often-difficult undertaking leaves many supervisors in a quandary.

This Manual is a practical tool to be used by supervisors and supervisees to assist them in incorporating a Multicultural Relational Perspective (MRP) into the supervisory process. We believe the establishment of an MRP is essential for the promotion of cultural awareness and sensitivity throughout the clinical process.

The Manual provides a roadmap for practicing and experienced supervisors to promote and integrate cultural sensitivity into the core of their work. It is not designed to provide an overview of the basic tenets of clinical supervision. Rather, the Manual presents a specialized version of supervision. Its focus is specifically geared towards highlighting the salient components of the supervisory process that must be considered when integrating multiculturalism and diversity into supervision practices.

The Manual is organized into four seamless interrelated sections that are essential to developing an MRP in supervision: 1) Conceptual Considerations; 2) Structural Considerations; 3) Strategies and Techniques; and 4) Evaluation Tools. The Conceptual Considerations section contains chapters that provide an overview of the assumptions and ideology that underpin an MRP. The Structural Considerations section provides the reader with a two-step process for establishing an effective supervisory relationship. The Strategies and Techniques section includes a variety of chapters designed to provide supervisors and supervisees with hands-on tools for navigating difficult diversity-related conversations in supervision and beyond, as well as an array of experiential exercises that supervisors can employ to enhance cultural sensitivity. The Evaluation Tools section provides sample instruments that can be implemented to evaluate the goals and objectives of the entire supervisory process. For the convenience of our readers, we have also included additional supervisory resources at the end of the Manual that we hope will be helpful to supervisors and supervisees.

Kenneth V. Hardy, PhD
Toby Bobes, PhD

 Permission to photocopy the entire page is granted wherever this icon appears.

Acknowledgments

The idea for this Manual emerged as we were editing our book, *Culturally Sensitive Supervision and Training: Diverse Perspectives and Practical Applications*. We were excited about the idea for creating a practical hands-on tool for supervisors and supervisees that would provide the "know how" to promote and integrate cultural sensitivity into the core of their work.

We are grateful to our editor, Elizabeth Graber, for her unrelenting support and her ability to always find a way to make the impossible possible. Without her support, this Manual would not have been possible.

Our thanks to our contributing authors for their generosity and commitment. Our heartfelt appreciation to Nancy Steiny for her commitment and vision for high-quality training. We are grateful to J. Leonardo de la O for his contribution and creativity in the pursuit of experiential learning. We thank Matthew Mock for his enthusiastic support and valuable contribution.

We thank Fifi Klein for her unwavering support and commitment to this project. We appreciate her creativity and tireless efforts, devotion, and patience every step of the way. We could not have done this without you! We also wish to thank Dhara Mehta-Desai for her talents, expertise, and willingness to take on whatever task was needed regardless of size or scope and to do so with dedication. This has truly been a team effort.

We also would like to sincerely express our gratitude to the team of educators that we leaned on heavily to provide us with critical feedback and direction during the earlier drafts of this Manual. Drs. Kiran Arora, Christiana Awosan, Yajaira Curiel, Ana Hernandez, and Christian Jordal, your feedback has been instrumental in the shaping of the finished product. Dr. Rona Preli, we would also like to thank you for your honest and astute review of the Manual and providing us with the type of poignant feedback that encouraged us to think a little more deeply about the material.

We wish to acknowledge our many students, supervisees and workshop participants whose questions and comments informed and shaped the development of this specialized version of supervision. We also thank our supervisors in training whose voices and personal stories inspired us and helped to shape our vision for this Manual.

And finally, but not insignificantly, we wish to thank our families for the boundless patience and support that each of you demonstrated while we took valuable family time off to complete this project.

Kenneth V. Hardy, PhD
Toby Bobes, PhD

Part I

CONCEPTUAL CONSIDERATIONS

Core Supervisor Competencies

Kenneth V. Hardy, PhD and Toby Bobes, PhD

Supervisors have the power and privilege and therefore the responsibility to deliberately initiate conversations about cultural diversity. Supervision should be "a deliberate educational process" with teaching and learning strategies that are proactive, purposeful, and intentional (Borders, 2001, pp. 417–418). The core competencies listed below, and throughout this chapter, are based upon these premises.

A more comprehensive coverage of these core competencies may be found in *Culturally Sensitive Supervision and Training: Diverse Perspectives and Practical Applications* (Hardy & Bobes, 2016).

1. Be a "broker of permission" to give voice to previously silenced topics.
2. Introduce dimensions of diversity in the initial supervision or class to set the tone to explicitly acknowledge and validate the lived experiences of group members of diverse backgrounds.
3. Explicitly name and address the impact of power relations and privilege upon relationships.
4. Engage in critical self-reflection and self-interrogation.
5. Expand on knowledge of self and deepen understanding of "Self in Relationship to Other."
6. Be alert to discomforts and emotional responses when diversity/multicultural issues arise.
7. Effectively manage culturally-based hot buttons or emotional triggers.
8. Promote awareness of and sensitivity to the anatomy of socio-cultural oppression.
9. Highlight, deconstruct, and make visible the invisible trauma wounds of socio-cultural oppression.
10. Embrace "Both-And Thinking."
11. Utilize the "Validate, Challenge, and Request Approach," a requisite skill for engaging in difficult dialogues.
12. Recognize that all relationships are cross-cultural.
13. Demonstrate the ability to hold meaningful and progressive conversations about culture and context.
14. Distinguish between awareness and sensitivity.
15. Be curious and sensitive about how language informs the supervisee's experiences.
16. Embrace a stance of compassion, humility, and curiosity.

17. Focus upon the multiple levels of interaction and interconnection at various systems levels.
18. Create culturally informed questions.
19. Embrace cultural diversity and social justice.
20. Differentiate between cultural diversity and social justice.

We believe the core competencies contribute significantly to the promotion of culturally sensitive and culturally competent supervision and training. Hardy and Laszloffy (1995) write:

> Training programs devoted to preparing culturally competent therapists must recognize and attend to the distinction between awareness and sensitivity. Awareness is primarily a cognitive function; an individual becomes conscious of a thought or action and processes it intellectually. Sensitivity, on the other hand, is primarily an affective function; an individual responds emotionally to stimuli with delicacy and respectfulness. Although these functions appear unique and separate, each is shaded with nuances of the other. Essentially, awareness involves a conscious sensitivity, and sensitivity involves a delicate awareness.

> *The unifying themes of these core competencies are thinking relationally, contextually, and culturally.*

MULTILAYERED REALITIES IN SUPERVISION

Thinking Relationally—Thinking Contextually/Culturally

Viewing the multilayered realities in supervision enhances our abilities to develop a larger conceptual framework for conducting supervision and to operationalize the core supervisor competencies. Developing a cognitive map or framework is an important "conceptual leap" so that supervisors are aware of what they are doing and why they are doing it (Borders, 1992).

The Multicultural Relational Perspective (MRP) is a worldview that provides an in-depth and comprehensive framework for clinical supervision. The MRP is a philosophical stance that is the conceptual foundation for this Manual. This approach is predicated on the premise that therapy and supervision are parallel processes and are organized around the following beliefs and values:

- The centrality of relationships and the notion that human suffering is located within relationships.
- That cultural factors are salient contextual variables in our lives and must be attended to with humility, sensitivity, and competence.

- That our understanding of socio-cultural trauma and the hidden wounds associated with it are essential to clinical effectiveness.
- That an acute exploration of the self of the therapist and self of the supervisor issues are critical to the provision of effective therapy and supervision.
- That clinicians explore and understand the role their biases (unconscious and otherwise) may have on therapy and supervision.

DEVELOPING SUPERVISION—A QUANTUM LEAP

Supervisors take a quantum leap in their development as they transition from being a therapist to being a supervisor. This shift requires a significant leap in thinking, skills, and professional identity (Steiny, 2010). Developing SuperVision requires extraordinary vision, the ability to look beyond what is spoken, make the invisible visible, and cast a wide net to continually search for all relevant contexts and meanings. In a sense, supervisors are visionaries, "people who look beyond the day-to-day routine" (Roberts, 2002, p. 335).

Developing SuperVision means to broaden our focus so that we are "thinking relationally," "thinking systemically," and "thinking contextually." We believe that an effective framework for conducting clinical supervision is one that is based on a more contextual understanding of ourselves, our supervisees, our society, our history, and our clients' lives (McGoldrick & Hardy, 2008). We need to keep context in view so that we work from a truly inclusive orientation. Viewing therapy and supervision from inclusive cultural perspectives offers "a sense of hope and belonging" (2008, p. xi) and a voice for all participants.

A CONCEPTUAL FRAMEWORK FOR SUPERVISION

Thinking Relationally

"Thinking Relationally" is an umbrella concept predicated on the belief in the centrality of relationships and the notion that human suffering is located within relationships. Super-vision interventions should be relationally based and reflect the supervisor's attunement to and emotional resonance with the needs and feelings of supervisees and clients, especially when working with those whose cultural backgrounds are different from their own.

Learning to *Think Relationally* is key to the development of an MRP. Supervisors can help promote and foster relational thinking by encouraging supervisees to continuously explore the connectedness and interactions between all matter, especially those that are often considered disparate. While the range of possibilities and potential foci for exploration are virtually infinite, we have identified 10 core domains of interest we routinely highlight in supervision. The **domains of interest** we emphasize to promote "Both/And" or relational thinking are as follows:

1. **Affect and Cognition**—Too often our work highlights one of these entities to the exclusion of the other. With regard to affect and cognition, the supervisee is

consistently encouraged to consider how each affects and is affected by the other. When one is elevated or scrutinized to the virtual exclusion of the other, the supervisee is encouraged to consider both the other as well as whatever underlying meaning, if any, that might be attached to why it has been excluded or marginalized. In adherence with the MRP, the supervisee is also encouraged to consider the role that both affect **and** cognition play at every level of the therapeutic-supervisory relationship.

2. **Past and Present**—The dichotomy between "past" and "present" is replete throughout the field. The dichotomy has informed theoretical approaches which either promote the saliency of "history" (the past) or the wisdom of looking forward and focusing on the "here and now" (the present). The MRP asserts that it is virtually impossible to disentangle the past and present, thus its focus is on the intersection of the two. The significance and implications of "the future" are also examined within this context as well.

3. **Health and Pathology**—The MRP stresses the importance of supervisors reminding supervisees of the potential interlocking dimensions of health and pathology. Thus it is important to help supervisees think critically and relationally about the ways in which there can be strands of health contained in pathology and vice versa.

4. **Ecology, Psychology, and Biology**—The use of each of these terms in this context is metaphorical. *Ecology* is used to refer to the socio-cultural context in which one is embedded. In other words, one's environment in the broadest sense of the word. *Psychology*, on the other hand, is used to refer to one's mind, i.e., one's mental, spiritual and/or psychological state. And finally, *Biology* refers to the (physical) body. In everyday life these three spheres of living are inextricably meshed. Being mindful of the interrelationship of these concepts in supervision is essential to the development of relational thinking and the MRP.

5. **Functional and Dysfunctional**—"Functional" and "dysfunctional" are often considered in rigidly segregated ways that frequently obscure the intricate intertwinement that can exist between the two concepts. The MRP recognizes that it is highly possible to have functionality embedded within a web of dysfunction, as well as dysfunction contained in functionality.

6. **Problems and Solutions**—Supervisors are encouraged to invite supervisees to think about "problems" *and* "solutions" within the scope of their clinical work rather than one or the other. More importantly, supervisees must be supported in thinking about the relationship between "problems and solutions" especially in terms of how each influences and is influenced by the other.

7. **Actions and Reactions**—Considering the synergistic interplay between "actions" and "reactions" is closely aligned with the relationship between problems and solutions. While these two phenomena are often treated dichotomously, there is a dynamic relationship between the two that is critical to consider.

8. **Verbal and Non-Verbal Communication**—Often the richness and complexity of the supervisory and clinical experiences are diminished by the inadvertent inattention to the wide range of communication present in the supervisory/clinical relationship. Considerable attention is often devoted to "what is being said" (verbal) with less attention focused on what is being kinetically expressed (non-verbal). An intentional focus on the relationship between verbal and non-verbal patterns of communication

greatly enhances the opportunities to explore connections between thoughts and feelings, actions and reactions, and so forth.

9. **Self and Other**—The notion of *self in relationship to other* (SIRO) is a foundational premise of the MRP. In many respects, it is a refutation of the belief that "the self" can be completely and rigidly segregated from "other." Instead SIRO asserts that "the self" is both separate from and potently connected to "other" with each affected by and affecting the other.

10. **Validate and Challenge**—Validation refers to the ability to see, acknowledge, and name the redeemable dimensions of one's being and/or behavior. In a sense it requires one to demonstrate the ability to see the "strength" that may be contained in someone's expression of "weakness." A Challenge within the context of the MRP is a verbal acknowledgment of a person's behavior or being that is often counter-productive to the achievement of their desired goals in a relationship. The MRP is predicated on the thesis that acts of Validation and Challenge must be interlinked. Ideally, Validation should at all times precede a Challenge and a Challenge should be ultimately supported by a Validation that provides a pathway for a Challenge, and so on.

The aforementioned domains of interest for promoting relational thinking are illustrative and subjective. Supervisors (and supervisees) are encouraged to modify and/or augment this list with concepts that may hold greater salience for them personally and/or their respective relationship.

THINKING CONTEXTUALLY

"Thinking Contextually" is a conceptual skill that enables us to view multilayered realities, perspectives, and experiences that are overlapping and interconnecting. Hardy and Laszloffy (2002) discuss the significance of context:

> "Context" refers to the sense of embeddedness we all have that helps define the nature of our existence. It is the various milieus, perspectives, and experiences that we all have that help define the nature of our existence. . . . There is a virtually inextricable relationship between context and reality, in that context shapes our reality and it defines and punctuates the meanings we attach to our lives. . . . An MCP [MRP], as is common with many systemically based approaches, places a high premium on the significance of context. Like many other family therapy approaches, it recognizes the salience of the familial context as a major meaning-making marker of one's subjective experience, and it emphasizes the dimensions of culture as major contextual variables to be considered as well.
>
> (2002, p. 571)

Supervisors continually look beyond the content of the case to the multilayered realities and contextual influences simultaneously impacting themselves, their supervisees, clients, and others in the therapeutic and supervisory systems.

For example, supervisors begin to think systemically *and* relationally when they shift their focus from the individual client to the system in which the case is embedded including the therapy and supervisory systems (Reichelt & Skjerve, 2013). This means looking beyond the case to incorporate the therapist's own ideas, beliefs, and unique abilities to help them be more effective with their clients (Todd & Storm, 2014). Supervisors shift their attention from doing therapy to focus upon helping therapists tap into their own talents, strengths, abilities, and perspectives in clinical decision-making.

We use the terms thinking "Contextually" and "Culturally" interchangeably to refer to a process whereby intentional and comprehensive consideration is given to the significant role contextual variables play throughout our lived experiences. They not only influence how we see ourselves and how we see others, but also how we believe others perceive us. Thinking contextually enables us to develop a deeper understanding of others and ourselves as well as how contextual variables are generally attached to meaning making. Critical **domains of interest** to promote contextual thinking are:

- Ethnicity
- Class
- Gender
- Race
- Religion
- Sexual Orientation
- Nationality
- Age
- Ability
- Regionality

This list is illustrative and should in no way be considered exhaustive. The order in which the variables appear is strictly random and is not intended to imply any particular significance of one variable over another. We believe that contextual thinking is optimally achieved when these variables are comprehensively considered and especially in relationship to each other. Supervisors and supervisees are encouraged to adjust, prioritize, and/or augment the list in whatever ways that might be necessary to accommodate their unique supervisory experience.

LOCATION OF SELF-ORIENTATION

An essential relational and executive skill for supervisors is to utilize the location of self-orientation, a fundamental component associated with opening the door to difficult dialogues (Watts Jones, 2010, 2016). Supervisors model identification of their social location by discussing how their cultural identities (i.e., gender, race, class, etc.) might influence therapy and supervision relationships. Location of self involves acknowledging our multiple selves and how we make them explicit.

Hardy (2016) further clarifies the Location or Use of Selves as an essential component of the MRP:

The Location or Use of "Self" refers to the facility with which one can draw from the knowledge one has of one's self that can be accessed as a potential interpersonal resource to promote connections. The Location or Use of "Self" is predicated on the effective use of "Self" disclosure which is an important component of an MRP.

(Hardy, 2016, p. 6)

A CONTEXT MAP

A *context map* is a visual representation of the overlapping and interconnecting spheres of influence that surround the life experiences of supervisors, supervisees, clients, and all voices in the therapeutic and supervisory systems. See Figures 1.1, 1.2, and 1.3 on the following pages. These multilayered realities shape and inform how we think and what we do as clinicians.

Using this context map as a resource has the potential to generate new areas of inquiry, expand conversations, and enable the ongoing search for all relevant contexts and details in the life experiences of ourselves and of those with whom we work. We must increase our abilities to manage multiple levels of complexity and to move discursively among the spheres of influence.

The following context maps illustrate the increasing complexity of the multilayered realities inherent in the multicultural relational perspective.

AN APPLICATION OF MULTILAYERED REALITIES IN SUPERVISION

——————————— VIGNETTE: Kathy and Dan ———————————

Kathy and Dan, an African American couple in their mid-forties, were referred by their physician to this community agency for help in dealing with their increasingly strained relationship. Linda, a 30-year-old White woman, met with Kathy and Dan for the initial intake session while the supervisor and team observed behind the one-way mirror. This supervision group of six had been working together for a year and comprised two White women, two Latin men, one Asian American woman, and one African American man. The supervisor, Ben, was White. Dan said they needed help in communication because Kathy was becoming more withdrawn from him, and he was frightened and felt powerless. While they were hopeful that medication for Kathy's depression would soon take hold, they needed help in getting through this challenging time. Kathy said, "I hope the treatments will help so we can get our life back." As the therapist listened to the couple respectfully and validated their concerns, the anxiety in the room diminished appreciably. Linda asked questions to expand the couple's relational context: *"What was your life like together before these current concerns surfaced? What was your life like together in your early years as a couple? What are your hopes and dreams for the future?"* After listening to the session for a while, Ben called Linda in for a consultation because he wanted to explore additional ways to expand the dialogue.

Figure 1.1 A Context Map

Multilayered Realities in Supervision

Thinking Relationally—Thinking Contextually

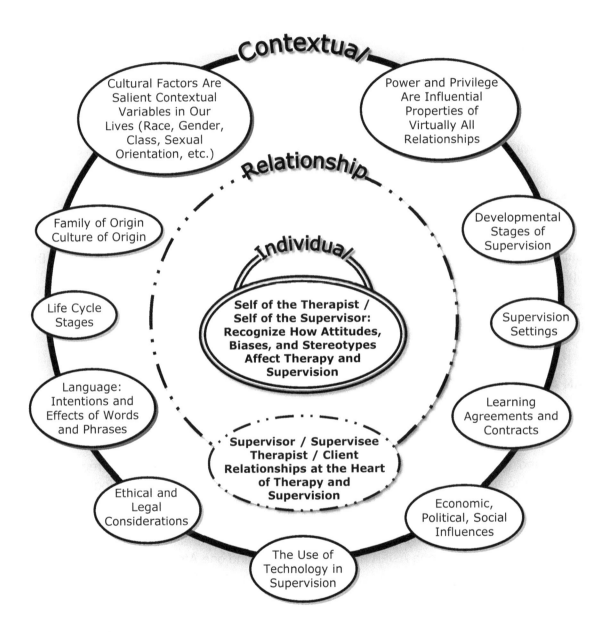

Figure 1.1 is a visual representation of the overlapping and interconnecting spheres of influence that surround the life experiences of supervisors, supervisees, clients, and all voices in the therapeutic and supervisory systems.

The creation of this Context Map was inspired by C. L. Murray and T. L. Murray who wrote The Couple's Resource Map in Solution-Focused Premarital Counseling: Helping Couples Build a Vision for Their Marriage (July, 2004) *Journal of Marital and Family Therapy*.

Figure 1.2 A Context Map with Increasing Complexity

Multilayered Realities in Supervision

Thinking Relationally—Thinking Contextually

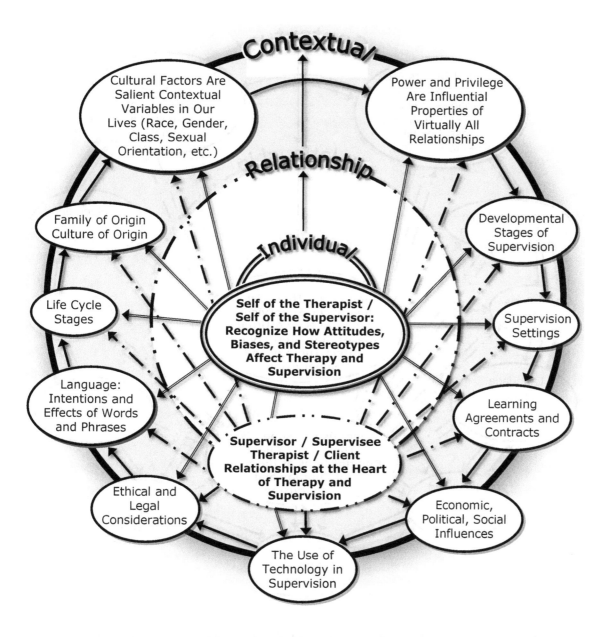

The arrows in Figure 1.2 illustrate the increasing complexity of multilayered realities in therapy and supervision relationships, as well as the socio-cultural influences that surround them.

The creation of this Context Map was inspired by C. L. Murray and T. L. Murray who wrote The Couple's Resource Map in Solution-Focused Premarital Counseling: Helping Couples Build a Vision for Their Marriage (July, 2004) *Journal of Marital and Family Therapy*.

Figure 1.3 A Context Map with Multidirectionality

Multilayered Realities in Supervision

Thinking Relationally—Thinking Contextually

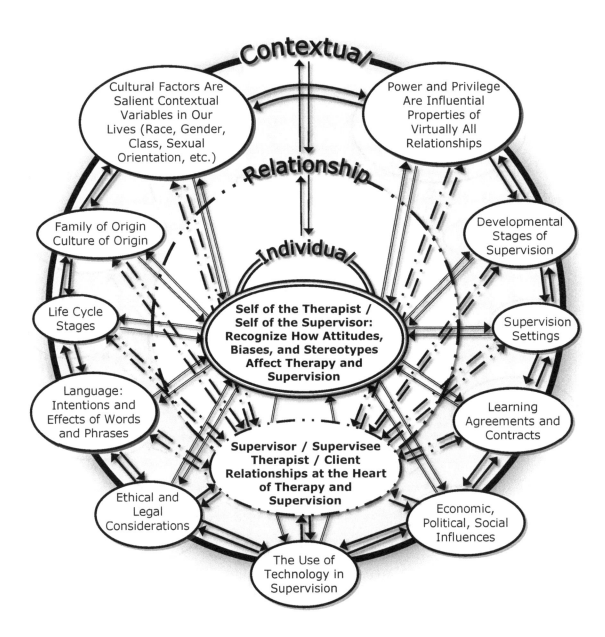

The arrows in Figure 1.3 illustrate the multidirectionality and reciprocal flow of therapy and supervision relationships as well as the socio-cultural influences that surround them. The figure is a visual representation of the inextricable connections and contextual details that influence the life experiences and multicultural realities of supervisors, supervisees, clients, and all voices in the therapeutic and supervisory systems.

The creation of this Context Map was inspired by C. L. Murray and T. L. Murray who wrote The Couple's Resource Map in Solution-Focused Premarital Counseling: Helping Couples Build a Vision for Their Marriage (July, 2004) *Journal of Marital and Family Therapy.*

Although the therapist, Linda, seemed calm during the therapy session, she revealed to the supervisory team her anxiety about working with a couple in which one partner was being treated for depression. After validating her concerns, Ben asked the group, "How would any of you work with this couple?"

The discussion that followed reflected the team's concerns, paralleling Linda's anxiety. Linda's intense reactivity was a reflection of the couple's anxiety. The reverberations rippled throughout the client, therapist, and supervisory systems. This isomorphic process generally occurs in all supervisory experiences. What is felt by the couple is experienced by the therapist and then transmitted to the team behind the mirror. The supervisor's role is to identify and bring this process to the consciousness of the entire group.[1]

———————— * * * ————————

Questions to Consider to Promote Discussion, Reflection, and Critical Thinking:

- What were your reactions to this vignette? What personal cultural triggers were evoked as you read the vignette?
- As the supervisor, how might you help Linda deepen her understanding of her anxiety and discomfort in working with this couple? What questions would you ask?
- As the supervisor, how might you help your supervisee use systemic interventions to more fully understand the relational context of this couple?
- In order to understand the broader systemic picture of the context of this client-couple, it would be helpful for the therapist to make contact with Kathy's physician to become familiar with the treatment plan for her depression. As the supervisor, how might you introduce the value of this systemic intervention to your supervisee? (The client-couple must give permission to make contact with Kathy's physician.)
- As the supervisor, how might you explore the similarities and differences between Linda and this couple that may influence the clinical work?
- How do individual differences of the supervisee, Linda, inform supervision (e.g., level of training, age, and life cycle stage)?

Note: Reference to Supervision Literature
Supervisors and therapists

> must be able both to conceptualize and to intervene at multiple levels and in multiple systems. . . . The multisystems levels include the individual, family subsystems, the family household, the extended family, nonblood kin, friends, church and community resources, social service agencies, and other outside systems.
>
> (Boyd-Franklin, 2003, pp. 227–228)

This chapter presented the key conceptual principles that are foundational in developing an MRP. The core competencies are built upon these principles and are germane to executing culturally sensitive supervision and training. Our primary focus is upon implementation and putting the principles into practice.

NOTE

1   This illustration of the isomorphic process is described by Bobes & Rothman (2002), p. 36.

REFERENCES

Bobes, T., & Rothman, B. (2002). *Doing Couple Therapy: Integrating Theory with Practice*. New York, NY: Norton.

Borders, L. D. (1992). Learning to Think Like a Supervisor. *The Clinical Supervisor, 10*(2), 135–148.

Borders, L. D. (2001). Counseling Supervision: A Deliberate Educational Process. In D. C. Locke, J. E. Meyers & E. L. Herr (Eds.), *The Handbook of Counseling* (pp. 417–432). Thousand Oaks, CA: SAGE Publications.

Boyd-Franklin, N. (2003). *Black Families in Therapy: Understanding the African-American Experience*. New York, NY: Guilford Press.

Hardy, K. V. (2016). Toward the Development of a Multicultural Perspective. In K. V. Hardy & T. Bobes (Eds.), *Culturally Sensitive Supervision and Training: Diverse Perspectives and Practical Applications* (pp. 3–10). New York, NY: Routledge.

Hardy, K. V., & Bobes, T. (Eds.). (2016). *Culturally Sensitive Supervision and Training: Diverse Perspectives and Practical Applications*. New York, NY: Routledge.

Hardy, K. V., & Laszloffy, T. A. (1995). The Cultural Genogram: Key to Training Culturally Competent Family Therapists. *Journal of Marital and Family Therapy, 21*(3), 227–237.

Hardy, K. V., & Laszloffy, T. A. (2002). Couple Therapy Using a Multicultural Perspective. In A. Gurman (Ed.), *Clinical Handbook of Couple Therapy* (pp. 569–593). New York, NY: Guilford Press.

McGoldrick, M., & Hardy, K. V. (Eds.). (2008). *Re-Visioning Family Therapy: Race, Culture and Gender in Clinical Practice* (2nd ed.). New York, NY: Guilford Press.

Murray, C. E., & Murray, T. L. (2004). Solution-Focused Premarital Counseling: Helping Couples Build a Vision for their Marriage. *Journal of Marital and Family Therapy, 30*(3), 349–358.

Reichelt, S., & Skjerve, J. (2013). The Reflecting Team Model Used for Clinical Group Supervision Without Clients Present. *Journal of Marital and Family Therapy, 39*(2), 244–255.

Roberts, J. (2002). Reflecting Processes and "Supervision": Looking at Ourselves as we Work with Others. In T. C. Todd & C. L. Storm (Eds.), *The Complete Systemic Supervisor: Context, Philosophy, and Pragmatics* (pp. 334–348). Lincoln, NE: Authors Choice Press.

Steiny, N. (2010) [1998]. Collaborative Training Tools for Supervisors and Supervisees. In *Practical Applications in Supervision*. California Association of Marriage and Family Therapists.

Todd, T. C., & Storm, C. L. (2014). Core Premises and a Framework for Systemic/Relational Supervision. In T. C. Todd & C. L. Storm (Eds.), *The Complete Systemic Supervisor: Context, philosophy, and Pragmatics* (2nd ed.). Malden, MA: Wiley.

Watts Jones, T. D. (2010). Location of Self: Opening the Door to Dialogue on Intersectionality in the Therapy Process. *Family Process, 49*(3), 405–420.

Watts Jones, T. D. (2016). Location of Self in Training and Supervision. In K. V. Hardy & T. Bobes (Eds.), *Culturally Sensitive Supervision and Training: Diverse Perspectives and Practical Applications*. New York, NY: Routledge.

2

A Developmental Model of Personal and Professional Growth

Toby Bobes, PhD

The premise of the developmental perspective is that the supervisor, supervisee, and the supervisory relationship grow, evolve, and change over time. Supervisors find that this perspective makes intuitive sense, and it offers a useful conceptual framework for planning supervision sessions, setting goals, and tailoring the supervision to meet the unique needs of supervisees (Campbell, 2006).

While our developmental model of personal and professional growth includes the beginning, intermediate, and advanced stages of supervision, we wish to note the fluidity of movement between the stages. The supervisor's roles, cultural tasks, strategies, and questions are designed to meet the particular learning needs of the supervisee. The supervisor's role shifts as supervision conversations expand upon the experiences and ideas generated in previous stages.

Our developmental model of supervision is based upon the principles of the Multicultural Relational Perspective (MRP) outlined and discussed in the first section of this Manual. Our model is both descriptive with respect to supervision processes and prescriptive with respect to questions posed as interventions.[1] It is our intention to assist supervisors to develop a culturally sensitive lens for both conceptualizing and intervening with essential skills that are proactive, purposeful, and intentional.

BEGINNING STAGE: CREATING A SUPERVISION RELATIONSHIP: PROMOTING CULTURAL SENSITIVITY, TRUST, AND SAFETY

Strategies

Supervisors establish safety, structure, and direction. The supervisor's roles are educator, collaborator, and cultural facilitator. The supervisor's cultural tasks are to:

- Assist the supervisee with refining his or her thinking about the importance of culture
- Help the supervisee understand self as a cultural being
- Invite supervisees to consider the ways in which their cultural selves shape how they interact in supervision and therapy

- Establish an explicit supervision contract which details the agreement between the supervisor and supervisee for working together

Supervisors clarify their expectations, and they tailor interventions to the learning needs and goals of supervisees. They help supervisees state their goals. These goals should have identifiable benchmarks so that the supervisor and supervisee will be able to experience concrete, measurable success in their work together (Steiny, 2010). It is helpful to use learning goals to guide the supervisor's ongoing feedback and evaluation of the supervisee.

Supervisors promote a climate of safety, risk-taking, and transparency in dialogues. They invite conversations with supervisees to dialogue about their cultural identities such as race, gender, class, sexual orientation, and religion. Supervisors introduce dimensions of diversity in the initial supervision session to set the tone to explicitly acknowledge and validate the lived experiences of group members of diverse backgrounds. They model identification of their social location and invite thoughtfulness and dialogue about the explicit and implicit ways that power, privilege, and subjugation operate in therapy, supervision, and training contexts (Watts Jones, 2010).

Supervisors utilize "The VCR Approach, the Art and Skill of Validating and Challenging." Validating the supervisee sufficiently is a critical first step that must precede any form of challenge or confrontation. Validation means sending a message that conveys, "I understand your perspective—I recognize where you're coming from." It is important to make the distinction that validation is not synonymous with agreement. By recognizing this critical distinction, it becomes much easier to offer validation (Hardy & Laszloffy, 2007, p. 151). The VCR Approach is outlined and discussed in the *Strategies and Techniques* section of this Manual.

Supervisors invite supervisees to introduce themselves culturally: "Describe something you like most about your cultural background and something you find hardest to deal with" (Hardy & McGoldrick, 2008, p. 454). The supervisor shares his or her experience first. The use of self through cultural sharing, or telling one's own story, is a powerful way for supervisors to connect to learners' lived experiences. Group members experience increased connection and become more engaged as they introduce themselves culturally.

Questions as Interventions in the Beginning Stage of Supervision:

- What would you like to get from our supervision experience?
- How might I be helpful to you as you begin to see clients?
- Let's talk about your previous supervision experiences. Which ones have worked for you and which ones have not worked so well? This will enable us to understand what to do more of and what to do differently.
- "I really want this to be an open process between us. I am inviting you to let me know if there is any time that I say or do something that makes you feel uncomfortable or if you are even wondering why I say or ask you something. I will also check in with you from time to time to see if we are doing OK" (Lappin & Hardy, 2002, p. 42).

- Are you aware of particular situations that may lead to discomfort for you? For example, clinical dilemmas that may be beyond your comfort zone?
- As a supervisor, I have the responsibility for helping supervisees state clear goals for their supervision experience. What are some of your learning goals for yourself as a therapist?

Culturally Informed Questions to Ask in Beginning and All Stages of Supervision:

- How do you define/describe yourself as a cultural being?
- Of the various dimensions of self, including but not limited to race, gender, class, sexual orientation, which dimensions are easy to own and embrace/not easy to own and embrace?
- Which dimensions of your self are sources of your greatest personal discomfort/ sources of your personal pride?
- Of the range of differences, including but not limited to race, gender, class, sexual orientation, which kinds of difference are you most comfortable with/most uncomfortable with?
- How might these personal experiences of difference shape how you interact in supervision and therapy?
- How does your culture shape and inform your attitudes and beliefs about privilege and power?

INTERMEDIATE STAGE: EXPAND AND DEEPEN SUPERVISORY CONVERSATIONS: FACILITATING CULTURALLY SENSITIVE DIALOGUES

Strategies

Supervisors increase sensitivity to contextual influences and expand awareness of the impact of power and privilege upon therapy and supervision relationships. The supervisor's roles are cultural facilitator and collaborator. The supervisor's cultural tasks are to:

- Assist supervisee to expand on knowledge of self as a cultural being and deepen understanding of "Self in Relationship to Other."
- Invite supervisee to have an unrelenting commitment to remain curious—not just about "the other" but also about one's own perceptions, feelings, and reactions.
- Model "Context-Talk" so that supervisee develops the fluency and comfort to speak openly, non-defensively, and routinely about culture and context.
- Focus on strengths and build confidence of supervisee.
- Encourage effective therapist use of self and development of therapeutic skills and competencies.

Supervisors have the power and privilege and therefore the responsibility to deliberately initiate conversations about cultural diversity. Supervisors model identification of their social location and invite supervisees to share relevant aspects of their cultural identities. This conversation is one way of addressing power differences in the supervisory relationship (Porter, 2014).

Supervisors monitor emotional responses when diversity and multicultural issues arise. Supervisors bear the primary responsibility for working through emotional discomfort when it inevitably arises during conversations about multicultural differences (Christiansen, et al., 2011). Staying with the intensity in the moment is critical in facilitating emotionally charged conversations.

Supervisors utilize the "VCR Approach, the Art and Skill of Validating and Challenging." This approach is used at all stages of supervision.

Supervisors invite self-reflection at all stages of supervision. Engaging in critical self-reflection enables us to get more intimately acquainted with ourselves as cultural beings. It is a "looking-within process" in which we have the opportunity to examine deeply held internalized views about racial, gender, ethnic, and sexual differences. Expanding on knowledge of self through self-reflection and deepening understanding of self in relation to other are core competencies that are interwoven throughout supervision and therapy.

Culturally Informed Questions to Ask at Intermediate and All Stages of Supervision:

- As we work together, would you let me know if I say something to you that suggests that I do not understand your experience?
- In working with clients of different cultural backgrounds, we need to be aware of our own experiences and attitudes about difference. Can you think about a time in your life when you felt "different from" or devalued? It may be a difference related to race, gender, class, or sexual orientation. It can be in current time or in a previous time in your life. The supervisor shares his or her experience first (Hardy & Bobes, 2016).
- Let's look at how your gender, race, class, etc. may be affecting your interaction with this couple/family. What are your thoughts?
- How do you think the differences or sameness in our relationship may factor into our work together? (Lappin & Hardy, 2002).

Some Questions to Ask to Facilitate the Evaluation Process of Supervision:

- Let's take some time now to review how the supervision is going for you. What are you learning? What are you finding most useful?
- What are some of your learning goals that have been met so far?
- Are there some new learning goals that you think would broaden and deepen your work as a therapist?
- Will you identify some of your emerging strengths as a therapist?
- What are some of your successes as a therapist as you have tried out new therapy skills?

ADVANCED STAGE: INTEGRATION AND SYNTHESIS

The supervisor's role shifts into one of consultant and colleague as the supervisee integrates and synthesizes the supervision experience. The supervisor encourages articulation of the supervisee's integration and synthesis with particular focus upon the therapeutic use of self, acquired therapeutic skills, and the development of a culturally sensitive lens. The supervisor and supervisee have the opportunity to deepen their discussion about their relationship by experiencing *in vivo* the very phenomena and concepts they have addressed during their work together. Through mutual sharing, they explore and increase their understanding about the role their biases (unconscious and otherwise) may have on interactions in therapy and supervision.

The supervisor encourages risk-taking and provides new challenges. The supervisor invites the supervisee to state his or her learning goals for this last stage of their work together.

Questions to Ask at the Advanced Stage of Supervision:

- What are some of your strengths and learning challenges?
- How do you integrate what you *do* as a therapist with your preferred theoretical model?
- How does your preferred model of therapy incorporate the principles of the MRP?
- What competencies do you need to focus on in order to develop further your skills as a therapist?
- What are your thoughts about what actions you will take to enrich and promote your future professional development?

(AAMFT Handbook, 2015, p. 34)

Our developmental model of supervision is based upon the principles of the MRP and is designed to assist supervisors to tailor interventions to the learning needs and goals of supervisees. We find it useful to focus upon particular questions as interventions at the beginning, intermediate, and advanced stages of supervision. This developmental model of personal and professional growth assists supervisors to develop a culturally sensitive lens for intervening with essential skills that are proactive, purposeful, and intentional.

NOTE

1   The Integrated Developmental Model, the most widely used developmental model of supervision, is "both descriptive with respect to supervisee processes and prescriptive with respect to supervisor interventions" (Bernard & Goodyear, 2014, p. 35).

REFERENCES

AAMFT Handbook. (2015). American Association of Marriage and Family Therapy.

Bernard, J. M., & Goodyear, R. K. (2014). *Fundamentals of Clinical Supervision* (5th ed.). Upper Saddle River, NJ: Pearson Education.

Campbell, J. M. (2006). *Essentials of Clinical Supervision*. Hoboken, NJ: Wiley.

Christiansen, A. T., Thomas, V., Kafescioglu, N. et al. (2011). Multicultural Supervision: Lessons Learned about an Ongoing Struggle. *Journal of Marital and Family Therapy, 37*(1), 109–119.

Hardy, K. V., & Bobes, T. (Eds.). (2016). *Culturally Sensitive Supervision and Training: Diverse Perspectives and Practical Applications*. New York, NY: Routledge.

Hardy, K. V., & Laszloffy, T. A. (2007). *Teens Who Hurt: Clinical Interventions to Break the Cycle of Adolescent Violence*. New York, NY: Guilford Press.

Hardy, K. V., & McGoldrick, M. (2008). Re-Visioning Training. In M. McGoldrick & K. Hardy (Eds.), *Re-Visioning Family Therapy: Race, Culture, and Gender in Clinical Practice* (2nd ed.) (pp. 442–460). New York, NY: Guilford Press.

Lappin, J., & Hardy, K. V. (2002). Keeping Context in View: The Heart of Supervision. In T. C. Todd & C. L. Storm (Eds.), *The Complete Systemic Supervisor: Context, Philosophy, and Pragmatics* (pp. 41–58). Lincoln, NE: Authors Choice.

Porter, N. (2014). Women, Culture, and Social Justice: Supervision across the Intersections. In C. A. Falender, E. P. Shafranske & C. J. Falicov (Eds.), *Multiculturalism and Diversity in Clinical Supervision* (pp. 59–82). Washington, DC: American Psychological Association.

Steiny, N. (2010) [1998]. Collaborative Training Tools for Supervisors and Supervisees. In *Practical Applications in Supervision*. California Association of Marriage and Family Therapists.

Watts Jones, T. D. (2010). Location of Self: Opening the Door to Dialogue on Intersectionality in the Therapy Process. *Family Process, 49*(3), 405–420.

3

Race Through a Trauma Lens

Kenneth V. Hardy, PhD

Historically, there has been very little consideration given throughout the field to the interrelatedness of culture, oppression, and trauma. The field's insistence on rather narrow and lineal definitions of trauma has impeded our ability to fully grasp the pervasive and multitudinous ways in which trauma permeates the lives of marginalized groups. While it may not be uncommon for a clinician to astutely identify traumatic experiences within the interactional patterns of an immigrant family, for example, it would be uncommon for that same clinician to consider the very process of immigration through a prism of trauma. When culture is considered within the context of trauma, or trauma considered within the context of culture, the underlying dynamics are usually the same. The mindset is usually one that posits that "culture and trauma" are two discrete entities that may be related under some circumstances. It is rare, if ever, that aspects of culture, especially (socio-cultural) oppression, is conceptualized as a form of trauma. The failure to consider socio-cultural oppression as a manifestation of trauma, and trauma as a manifestation of socio-cultural oppression, has made it difficult, if not impossible, for clinicians and supervisors to respond effectively to the complex and multifaceted needs of many clients from oppressed backgrounds. Clients from marginalized and oppressed backgrounds are often misunderstood, misdiagnosed, and consequently underserved. The bifurcation of culture and trauma, and by extension, socio-cultural oppression, has made it difficult for many clinicians to conceptualize and respond appropriately to the oppression-related subtleties that often underpin and undermine effective clinical engagement and treatment. A much more expansive and broader notion of trauma is necessary, particularly one that highlights the dynamics of oppression.

THE PHENOMENA OF RACE AND TRAUMA

Expanding our notions regarding trauma is an idea whose time has arrived. For too long the issues of race and trauma have been viewed as separate entities. Scholars interested in race have spent considerable time discussing the relationship between race and oppression, but have devoted scant attention to the issue of trauma. Although much of this work has reflected an implicit understanding of the rudiments of trauma, it has not been addressed overtly. Promoting a more comprehensive understanding of the dynamics of racial oppression, as a form of trauma, is a necessary precursor to working with the racially marginalized.

Racial trauma is a life-altering and debilitating experience that affects countless numbers of individuals, families, and groups over multiple generations. It is an affirmation of the interlocking of racial oppression and trauma—the same experiences by different names. The tendency in the field to separate the two phenomena severely limits our collective understanding and ability to work with those who currently live life along the margins of society by virtue of their racial location. Racial trauma is the inescapable by-product of persistent direct or indirect exposure to repressive circumstances that have emotionally, psychologically, and/or physically devastated one's being and sense of self while simultaneously overwhelming, destroying, or neutralizing one's strategies for coping. Because by definition racial oppression is a systemic condition that is sustained and intense, occurring over a protracted period of time, there is very little release or relief from racial trauma. People of Color and members of other oppressed groups live in the midst of socio-cultural conditions that are injurious to their psyches and souls. Thus, even when clinical work is trauma informed, it is often oblivious to the subtle but potent impact of racial oppression and is frequently remiss in meeting the needs of those being served.

Race and racial trauma, for many People of Color, are integral aspects of culture. Racial trauma is an umbrella term that refers to experiences of domination-induced marginalization that results in the subjugation of a person or group based on their racial location. When thinking racially, everyone has exposure to racial trauma. While everyone of all races may have exposure to racial trauma, the actual experience one has depends on one's racial location and whether one is racially privileged or subjugated. No Person of Color is ever technically immune from some form of racial trauma, especially since a major feature of it has to do with being on the receiving end of the domination-subjugation cycle, particularly in response to one's racial location. Whites, on the other hand, by virtue of possessing racial privilege are often connected to the structures of racial domination that malign the lives of People of Color. The privilege of racial privilege is to have it and not know you have it, which can fuel acts of entitlement, domination, and oppression.

The realities of subjugation, on the other hand, are to live a life of psychological incarceration with underlying feelings of anger, suppressed rage, despair and humiliation. The process of subjugation is one of the many defining features of racial trauma. It is systemic and pervasive in its reach and affects all aspects of the lives of those who are racially targeted. Both DeGruy Leary (2005) and Hardy (1995) have discussed the ways in which the institution of slavery has forever and profoundly affected the everyday contemporary lives of many African Americans although they, themselves, were never slaves. According to DeGruy Leary, contemporary African Americans suffer from the trauma of Post Traumatic Slavery Syndrome.

DEVELOP A TRAUMA-INFORMED LENS

It is imperative for clinicians and supervisors of all races to possess a good working knowledge of race through a trauma-informed lens. It is important for Whites to understand their relationship, as Whites, to the broader experiences of racial oppression and trauma.

While it may be that an individual White person has not actively participated in the subjugation of People of Color, it is critical for that same White person to understand the inescapable ways in which "being white" is not just an individual identity as many Whites often suppose. However, it is also an identity that is an integral part of a larger group identity that is inextricably connected to a broader system of racial categorization, systematic oppression, and systemic racism. On the other hand, it is equally important for People of Color to understand how so much of their lives have been shaped by unacknowledged, unexamined exposure to and experiences with racial trauma.

The following questions can be quite useful in assisting supervisors and supervisees to explore the role of racial trauma in their lives as well as the lives of their clients. The questions can be used in individual, dyadic, or group supervision. The questions are designed to provoke critical thinking, encourage self-disclosure and self-interrogation, and to facilitate comfort, ease, and a developing expertise in talking about race.

Questions for Promoting Conversations about Race and Racial Trauma in Supervision:

1. At what age did you begin to think of yourself racially? Please describe the experience that highlighted this awareness for you.
2. What are two positive memorable racially based memories that you have and will never forget?
3. In what way has your racial identity (or how you identify racially) influenced how you see or think of yourself as a person and clinician/supervisor?
4. In what way has your racial identity (or how you identify racially) influenced how you believe others see you—as a person and as a clinician/supervisor?
5. Do you believe that one can be traumatized racially? Please use your personal experience(s) as a resource to help support your answer.
6. What is an emotional, behavioral, or psychological "symptom(s)" that you would associate with racial trauma?
7. What are some of the ways in which racial privilege might make it hard to "see" some of the emotional, psychological, or behavioral symptoms that could be associated with racial trauma?
8. How do you see yourself as a racial being?
9. What are two painful or regrettable racially based memories that you have and hope you can someday forget?
10. If you could ask one question to help you explore the depths of racial trauma experienced by someone, what question would you ask?

This chapter highlighted the significant and interlocking nature of racial oppression and trauma. Sample "starter questions" that incorporate the integration of racial trauma and oppression were provided to assist supervisors and trainees in both conceptualizing and discussing the critical intersection of race and trauma.

REFERENCES

DeGruy Leary, J. (2005). *Posttraumatic Slave Syndrome: America's Legacy of Enduring Injury and Healing*. Milwaukie, OR: Uptone Press.

Hardy, K. V. (1995). *The Psychological Residuals of Slavery*. San Francisco, CA: Psychotherapy.net.

4

"Naming It and Claiming It"—
Embracing Your Identity as an Activist
(Supervisor, Educator, Therapist)

Kenneth V. Hardy, PhD

I believe that therapists, supervisors, and educators have a role in promoting social justice, equity, and fairness in the wider community. Embracing one's identity as an activist means turning responsibility into defined action (Caldwell, 2016). Just as human rights activists are committed to helping others enhance the quality of their lives, we recognize and are sensitive to the powerful connection between relational struggles and the sociocultural context in which they are embedded (Hardy, 2001). This stance is summarized (p. 21):

> As family therapy educators, my colleagues and I are passionately committed to training therapists who are equipped to assist couples and families with their struggles of everyday life. In our unrelenting quest to accomplish such a goal, we constantly remind our students to think about couples, families, and the experience of suffering in broad, complex ways. Thus the skills that we endeavor to teach, as well as the wisdom we hopefully impart, is never divorced from the larger sociocultural context.

We now turn our attention to a communication competency which I will describe and illustrate.

"Naming it and claiming it" means giving language to the larger forces that shape people's lives but that remain unacknowledged and unnamed. It is essential that supervisors learn the power of giving language to something that had been previously unnamed. How can one possibly heal from a condition that has no name?

Educators and practitioners routinely refer to the DSM to locate the "professional shorthand" and best terms to fit the circumstances of their clients. However, these are terms that are limiting and confine the boundaries of our understanding to a naming process that is based upon the medical model. *There are no terms in the DSM that capture the invisible forces that profoundly shape our lives—such as psychological homelessness, devaluation, and voicelessness.*

DEMONSTRATION OF A THERAPIST'S USE OF SELF: EMBRACING A NEW IDENTITY AS BOTH AN ACTIVIST AND A THERAPIST

Adapted from "The View from Black America: Listening to the Untold Stories" (Hardy, 2015)

As my awareness of the challenge of helping poor people deal with having the odds so stacked against them by their social circumstances grew, I embraced a new identity as both an activist and a therapist. I learned to see my role as helping community members "name it and claim it"—to see beyond themselves to understand how factors like racism and poverty were part of the problems they were struggling with. I saw my role as helping them take ownership of their rage, while recognizing that it's a larger problem they share with people in the same circumstances. It's like changing a negative to a positive. Rather than just being a passive victim, "naming it and claiming it" meant doing something proactive: it meant taking personal responsibility for one's life while giving language to a wider unfairness, which would otherwise be disregarded as a mysteriously invisible force.

The therapeutic value of this way of looking at things came into focus for me through a struggle my agency was having with a volatile man named Mr. Jordan, the father of four children and well known in the community as an especially tough character. He'd gone ballistic at the suggestion that he should give us permission to enroll his two youngest sons, Jason and Jarod, in a mentoring program. In a meeting with an agency team, he'd begun yelling, "My sons don't need no goddamn program like that. They got a mentor—me!" In the face of his diatribe, the team had backed down. Afterward, the majority view was that we should have hung tough and challenged Mr. Jordan more directly. As far as I could see, his confrontational skills were far beyond anything we could muster, even as a team. Something in the way I was beginning to see things compelled me to stick my neck out, and I volunteered to meet with Mr. Jordan alone.

After some subtle begging on my part, he agreed to give me no more than 15 minutes if I came out to see him. Standing in his doorway, I began by saying how much I appreciated his standing up for his kids, and as I said that, I thought I saw his shoulders drop an inch. "When I was a kid," I continued, "I always wanted my dad to stand up for me, but I knew that if he did that with White people, he'd be called an angry black man. Sometimes, I think black fathers can't win. They're either not involved enough, or they're too controlling."

At this point, Mr. Jordan looked directly at me for the first time and said, "Man, it's a bitch out there. If the White man ain't got his foot up your ass, he's trying to keep you down some other way. I got to deal with that shit at work every day. If it ain't the snooty White customers treating me like shit, it's the boss acting like I'm his property. One of these days, I'm gonna snap."

"I know what you mean," I found myself saying. "I snapped at my boss once, and it cost me my job. That's why black people have to think twice about taking that route. And brother, you especially have to be cool about it, because you have four little ones looking up to you. Goodness knows they need their dad to get through the world."

For the first time, Mr. Jordan smiled faintly. He then said, "Yeah, that's why I couldn't go along with that mentoring bullshit. It's like saying I can't be a father to my own boys."

"Look, your kids are lucky to have you as a father," I told him. "But the program isn't about dissing you as a father. It's just the opposite: it's about brothers coming together to help other brothers. Dads like you who have to work a lot of hours need someone available to pinch-hit when you're not around, to keep the gangbangers and drug dealers away from Jason and Jarrod while you're at work."

Our 15 minutes stretched into an hour. By the end, Mr. Jordan assured me, "I'll give it some serious thought. Maybe it could be good for them."

Virtually everything I did during my encounter with Mr. Jordan was counter to how I'd been trained and how I was supposed to conduct therapy at the clinic. I not only used my personal experiences with my dad to enter into Mr. Jordan's world as a black father, but openly shared my personal story about being fired, not to mention freely introducing the forbidden topic of race into the conversation, realizing that much of Mr. Jordan's determination to be a super dad was driven by his need to refute the largely pejorative social narrative about black fathers. Underneath the anger and the profanity, he was making a powerful statement that needed to be validated: "I am *not* a bad father!"

During our conversation I made myself present in a way I hadn't previously done with other clients. I was finding a voice that had been dormant in my formal training, with its narrow focus on diagnostic thinking and psychological functioning. I needed to learn to trust myself and my own experience to go beyond that limiting lens, to take into account the forces that molded the battle-hardened outlook of clients like Mr. Jordan. I'd reached a turning point in my development as a therapist: I was finally recognizing that to connect deeply with black people, I had to give the invisible wounds of racial trauma their due.

Concluding Remarks and Take-Aways

Our comprehensive framework for supervision is predicated on the premise that therapy and supervision are parallel processes. An acute exploration of self of the therapist and self of the supervisor are therefore critical. Using one's personal experiences and stories to enter the world of our trainees and clients may stretch us beyond our usual comfort zones. However, this way of working is key to providing culturally sensitive supervision and training.

Recommendations for Supervisors' Use of Selves

1. The supervisory relationship replicates a power dynamic in our society. Supervisors recognize that they have the power and privilege and therefore assume a greater responsibility to the relationship.
2. Supervisors acknowledge who they are with respect to their social locations and give language for how they might position themselves.

27

3. Supervisors name and claim their identities without putting the burden on supervisees or clients.
4. Supervisors address issues of oppression and social location and teach the location of self-orientation.
5. All supervisors self-interrogate and understand the significance of their racial identities for themselves and for whom they work. For example, White supervisors claim their whiteness, blind spots, and ignorance.

While self-disclosure may initially create tension in the supervisory relationship, learning occurs over time. It's like taking a time-release capsule. There is a waiting period for the process to have its ultimate effectiveness.

The reader is referred to *Culturally Sensitive Supervision and Training: Diverse Perspectives and Practical Applications* for multiple examples of the supervisor's use of self and diverse approaches to the location of self-orientation in therapy and supervision.

REFERENCES

Caldwell, B. (2016). Balancing Culture, Context, and Evidence-Based Practices in Supervision. In K. V. Hardy & T. Bobes (Eds.), *Culturally Sensitive Supervision and Training: Diverse Perspectives and Practical Applications* (pp. 79–85). New York, NY: Routledge.

Hardy, K. V. (2001, January). Healing the World in Fifty-Minute Intervals: A Response to "Family Therapy Saves the Planet." *Journal of Marital and Family Therapy, 27*(1), 19–22.

Hardy, K. V. (2015). The View From Black America: Listening to the Untold Stories. *Psychotherapy Networker, 39*(6), 19–25, 46–48.

Part II

STRUCTURAL CONSIDERATIONS

Establishing an Effective Supervisory Relationship

A Two-Step Process

Kenneth V. Hardy, PhD and Toby Bobes, PhD

One of the ways to establish a viable and effective supervisory relationship from a Multi-cultural Relational Perspective (MRP) involves being explicit about one's philosophy of supervision and establishing a supervision contract. By doing so, the supervisor exercises leadership in making many of the implicit elements of supervision and the accompanying process explicit. Both the explication of the supervisor's philosophy and the execution of a contract help to clarify the expectations and rules of engagement that underpin the supervisory process. It also crystallizes the responsibilities of the supervisor and the ways in which she or he can be held accountable throughout the supervisory process.

In the first section of this chapter, **Statement of Supervision Philosophy**, we provide a list of questions relevant to core topic areas that supervisors might consider and find useful in articulating their philosophy of supervision. In the second section we present **A Sample Framework for Establishing an Explicit Supervision Contract** using an MRP. Since our goal is to provide a sample blueprint for incorporating the core principles and competencies of the MRP into a supervision contract, we have deliberately limited the components contained in our framework to those that are germane to this perspective. Our intent is to provide a sample framework for establishing a supervision contract that represents an augmentation of the myriad of contracts in the field and address supervision more generically. Thus, we have only included items in this framework that build on the existing literature and that are pertinent to promoting culturally competent supervision.

STATEMENT OF SUPERVISION PHILOSOPHY

The philosophy of supervision should clearly articulate the centrality of cultural sensitivity in the supervisory process. Articulating one's personal philosophy and model of supervision is a critical first step for supervisors in developing a framework for promoting and integrating cultural sensitivity into the core of their work. We have drawn from several sources in the existing literature to select the core topic areas.[1] The questions that accompany each topic area provide the opportunity for supervisors to begin to reflect upon and identify their assumptions, beliefs, values, and personal philosophy of supervision.

The following worksheets may be used as a guide in developing your personal philosophy and model of supervision.[2]

WORKSHEET 1

GETTING SUPERVISION OFF TO A GOOD START: CONTRACTS[3]

- When beginning supervision, whether individual or group, how do you get to know your supervisees? What are some of the ways you initially engage your supervisees?

- How do you introduce the concept of the supervision contract as a powerful and essential ingredient of an effective supervisory relationship?

- How do you invite collaboration with your supervisees in the development of the supervision contract?

- What are the components that you include in your supervision contract?

- How do you initiate conversations about diversity in this initial supervision session to promote a climate of safety, risk-taking, and transparency in dialogues?

_____

_____

_____

_____

_____

_____

_____

_____

_____

_____

_____

_____

_____

_____

_____

WORKSHEET 2

TAKING LEADERSHIP IN FACILITATING AND PROMOTING CULTURAL SENSITIVITY

- How do you take the lead in cultivating a safe learning environment?

- How do you take leadership in addressing and challenging all forms of oppression?

- To what extent do you encourage supervisees to explore the impact of power, privilege, and oppression within the auspices of their clients' lives and their relationship with clients? (Hardy, 2016)

- Under what clinical circumstances do you initiate conversations about the dimensions of culture?

- What role does the location of self-orientation play in your current philosophy of supervision?

- To what extent, if any, might you explore the multiple selves of the supervisee? How often do you encourage supervisees to consider how their multiple selves may impact their participation in supervision and their therapy with clients?

- What specific strategies do you employ to enhance cultural sensitivity in both your supervisory relationship as well as within the clinical work of your supervisees?

_____

_____

_____

_____

_____

_____

_____

_____

_____

_____

_____

_____

WORKSHEET 3

EXAMINING VARIOUS MODELS OF SUPERVISION

- What are some therapy and/or supervision models that have most influenced your supervision practices?[4]

- What are the similarities and differences between your model of therapy and your model of supervision?

- How has the work of various contributors to the field impacted your theory of therapy? Your theory of supervision?

- What are some of the ways in which the various models of supervision have fidelity to the multicultural perspective? In other words, how do the models use a culturally sensitive lens with a focus upon use of self as supervisor; consider the influence of power relations and privilege in therapy and supervision relationships?

- Which models of supervision place greater emphasis upon skills, strategies, and interventions? Which models are more likely to focus upon therapy and supervision relationships?

- Which models and methods are more congruent with your personal style?

_____

_____

_____

_____

_____

_____

_____

_____

_____

_____

_____

_____

_____

_____

WORKSHEET 4

THINKING ABOUT THERAPY AND SUPERVISION IN RELATIONAL TERMS

- How do you invite thoughtfulness and dialogue about the influence of power relations and privilege in supervision?

- How do you invite supervisees to reflect upon themselves as cultural beings and to deepen their understanding of "self in relationship to other?"

- What are your beliefs about the supervisor/supervisee hierarchy?

- How does systems thinking inform your supervision practice?

- Using a culturally sensitive lens, provide an example of the multiple systemic levels of client, therapist, and supervisor interaction occurring in the context in which you work.

- How do you facilitate understanding of systemic thinking in supervision? For example, how do you introduce concepts about circularity, patterns of connection, cultural context? Initiate exercises that illuminate the diversity of multiple voices in a system? Model circular questions?

- What are your experiences in making the important cognitive shift from thinking like a therapist to thinking like a supervisor? What are the ways in which you shift the focus from the family/couple, individual to the therapeutic and supervisory systems?

_____

_____

_____

_____

_____

_____

_____

_____

_____

_____

WORKSHEET 5

ARTICULATING YOUR BELIEFS ABOUT CHANGE

- What are your beliefs about how people grow and change?

- What is your theory about how change occurs?

- What are some of the ways that you as a supervisor use yourself to facilitate change in the context of supervision?

- What are your beliefs about the use of self as an agent of change in supervision? In therapy?

- What are some pivotal events in your personal life that have contributed to your beliefs about how change occurs?

_____

_____

_____

_____

_____

_____

_____

_____

_____

_____

_____

_____

_____

_____

_____

_____

_____

WORKSHEET 6

ENHANCING SENSITIVITY TO CULTURE AND CONTEXT

- How do you initiate conversations with supervisees about their cultural identities such as race, gender, class, sexual orientation, and religion?

- How do you model cultural sensitivity in supervision?

- How do you explicitly name and address the influence of power relations and privilege upon therapy and supervision relationships?

- How do you help supervisees to work with clients whose cultures and worldviews are different from their own?

- What are your beliefs about how the gender differences between supervisor and supervisee impact supervision?

- How do you introduce the concept of "the cultural context of behavior" into supervision conversations to increase understanding of the attitudes, beliefs, and behaviors of those with whom we work? For example, the cultural context of a supervisee or supervisor could refer as much to one's level of clinical experience and previous training as it does to one's ethnicity, race, sexual orientation or dimensions of diversity.

_____

_____

_____

_____

_____

_____

_____

_____

_____

_____

_____

_____

_____

WORKSHEET 7

ADDRESSING DIMENSIONS OF DIVERSITY DURING THE VARIOUS STAGES OF SUPERVISION

- How do you shape the conversation about diversity to the developmental stage of the supervisee?

- How do individual differences of the supervisee (e.g., level of training, age, and life cycle stage) inform supervision?

- How is your pursuit of the supervisee's cultural self shaped by his or her level of experience and stage of training?

_____

_____

_____

_____

_____

_____

_____

_____

_____

_____

_____

_____

_____

_____

_____

_____

_____

_____

_____

_____

WORKSHEET 8

SELECTING METHODS AND TECHNIQUES THAT PROMOTE CULTURAL SENSITIVITY

- What is your rationale for your choice of supervisory methods? How do the methods you choose facilitate achievement of your supervisory goals?

- What are the various methods and techniques that have been useful to you in promoting cultural sensitivity and competency in supervision?

- What are the factors most important to you in selecting methods and techniques?

- If you were designing a case presentation format, what are the salient points you would want to know about each case? What points would you be sure to include to promote cultural sensitivity?

- While it is *always* crucial to attend to supervisee anxiety in supervision, when the subject of "live" supervision comes up, anxiety increases dramatically for supervisors and supervisees. How do you set the stage for teamwork and prepare supervisees for a respectful, supportive learning experience? For example, be clear about supervisee goals for session, create understanding of team's role. What other learning agreements are important?

- What methods have you found useful to help supervisees recognize and explore their discomforts so that they will be more effective with their clients?

_____

_____

_____

_____

_____

_____

_____

_____

_____

_____

_____

_____

WORKSHEET 9

ADDRESSING CULTURALLY-BASED ETHICAL AND LEGAL DILEMMAS

- If you have a supervisee who refuses to provide services on religious grounds, or any other value system, how would you address and explore the issues?

- We believe that the hallmark for providing culturally sensitive supervision is to promote awareness and sensitivity for how one's cultural identities, values, and beliefs affect therapeutic and supervision practices. Thus we need to explore attitudes about difference in supervision and training. How do you promote awareness and sensitivity about difference in your supervision practices?

- As a supervisor, are there beliefs that you hold that preclude the provision of supervision to certain supervisees? If yes, what is your process for attending to these issues?

_____

_____

_____

_____

_____

_____

_____

_____

_____

_____

_____

_____

_____

_____

_____

_____

_____

_____

WORKSHEET 10

ARTICULATING KNOWLEDGE OF SUPERVISION LITERATURE

- Articulate how your supervision philosophy and methods relate to the current diversity informed supervision literature.

- What books and/or articles have enhanced your understanding of the MRP, use of self as supervisor, self of the therapist, and culturally sensitive supervision practices?

_____

_____

_____

_____

_____

_____

_____

_____

_____

_____

_____

_____

_____

_____

_____

_____

_____

_____

_____

_____

_____

_____

_____

A SAMPLE FRAMEWORK FOR ESTABLISHING AN EXPLICIT SUPERVISION CONTRACT

Establishing an explicit supervision contract details the agreement between the supervisor and supervisee for working together. A focused contract is a powerful and essential ingredient of a fruitful supervisory relationship. Clarifying expectations on both sides eliminates many potential pitfalls (Steiny, 2010). It is important to note the fluidity of the agreements made between supervisor and supervisee. This collaborative process may be renegotiated at any point to meet the learning needs of the supervisee. For example, once the learning goals of supervisees have been successfully met, this particular part of the contract disappears, and new learning goals are created (2010).

The supervisor holds the power, privilege, and assumes greater responsibility in the relationship by virtue of his or her role and position. Thus, the supervisor must be continually attuned to the supervisee's less powerful position and invite discussion about power differences at the initial supervision session. Making power relations visible demystifies the elusive nature of power in the supervision relationship and paves the way for goodwill, trust, and collaboration (Turner & Fine, 2002; Murphy & Wright, 2005). Transparency about power relations facilitates a more open conversation when addressing the components of the supervision contract.

Many supervisors assert the importance of written contracts to formalize agreements. Written contracts provide support and clarity about previous agreements especially when supervisees from their less powerful position wish to revisit and discuss a particular part of the process (Bernard & Goodyear, 2014; Storm & Todd, 2014). In this section we present broad process issues and components of supervision contracts that are essential in providing culturally sensitive supervision.

A Sample Framework

1. Mechanics of Supervision

    *   Logistics (date, time, compensation if relevant, etc.)
    *   Changes (time, membership, format, etc.)—any and all changes that impact the supervisory relationship and/or process will be discussed and negotiated when unanticipated variables come into play
    *   Supervisee Expectations and Responsibilities
    *   Supervisor Expectations and Responsibilities
    *   Format and Process of Evaluation

2. Making the Implicit Explicit

    *   Theory of Change
    *   Philosophy of Supervision
    *   Bias Safeguards such as Management of Transference/Countertransference and Acknowledgment of Cultural Triggers
    *   Deconstructing Power and Privilege in the Supervisory Relationship

3. Ethics

- Professional Ethics—adhere to ethics of profession
- Relational Ethics—how you value relationships in shared humanity

4. Critical issues that are highly relevant to culturally sensitive supervision should be discussed

- Therapist use of self(ves)
- Supervisor use of self(ves)
- Broker of Permission
- Context Talk
- Thinking Culturally/Contextually
- Impact of Power
- Impact of Privilege
- Understanding of Trauma and Oppression
- Self(ves) of the Therapist Considerations
- Establishing an Effective Supervisory Relationship

Establishing an effective supervisory relationship is central to providing culturally sensitive supervision. The **Statement of Supervision Philosophy** and **Establishing an Explicit Supervision Contract** are highly interrelated competencies that are built upon the key foundational principles of an MRP set forth in Chapter 1. The supervisor should be deliberate and proactive in his or her desire, intention, and effort to develop and enhance cultural sensitivity.

NOTES

1   AAMFT Handbook (2015) and Curriculum Guide for Training Counseling Supervisors: Rationale, Development, and Implementation (Borders, et al., 1991).
2   We wish to acknowledge Sharon Duffy, PsyD, who created the idea of a Supervision Paper Worksheet.
3   Nancy Steiny writes about "getting off to a good start" in supervision in her chapter in this Manual, "Collaborative Training Tools for Supervisors and Supervisees."
4   This question was adapted from "Family Therapy Supervision Theory-Building Questions" by F. P. Piercy and D. H. Sprenkle in *The Reasonably Complete Systemic Supervisor Resource Guide* (1997, p. 101).

REFERENCES

Approved Supervision Designation: Standards Handbook (June, 2015 Revision). American Association for Marriage and Family Therapy.

Bernard, J. M., & Goodyear, R. K. (2014). *Fundamentals of Clinical Supervision* (5th ed.). Upper Saddle River, NJ: Pearson Education.

Borders, L. D., Bernard, J. M., Dye, H. A., Fong, M. L., Henderson, P., & Nance, D. W. (1991). Curriculum Guide for Training Counseling Supervisors: Rationale, Development, and Implementation. In *Counselor Education and Supervision, 31*.

Hardy, K. V. (2016). Toward the Development of a Multicultural Relational Perspective in Training and Supervision. In K. V. Hardy & T. Bobes (Eds.), *Culturally Sensitive Supervision and Training: Diverse Perspectives and Practical Applications* (pp. 3–10). New York, NY: Routledge.

Murphy, M. J., & Wright, D. W. (2005). Supervisees' Perspectives of Power Use in Supervision. *Journal of Marital and Family Therapy, 31*(3), 283–295.

Piercy, F. P., & Sprenkle, D. H. (1997). Family Therapy Supervision Theory-Building Questions. In C. L. Storm & T. C. Todd (Eds.), *The Reasonably Complete Systemic Supervisor Resource Guide.* Needham Heights, MA: Allyn & Bacon.

Steiny, N. (2010) [1998]. Collaborative Training Tools for Supervisors and Supervisees. In *Practical Applications in Supervision.* California Association of Marriage and Family Therapists.

Storm, C. L., & Todd, T. C. (2014). Developing Contextually Informed Best Practices in Systemic Supervision. In T. C. Todd & C. L. Storm (Eds.), *The Complete Systemic Supervisor: Context, Philosophy, and Pragmatics* (2nd ed.). Malden, MA: Wiley.

Turner, J., & Fine, M. (2002). Gender and Supervision: Evolving Debates. In T. C. Todd & C. L. Storm (Eds.), *The Complete Systemic Supervisor: Context, Philosophy, and Pragmatics* (pp. 72–80). Lincoln, NE: Authors Choice Press.

Part III

STRATEGIES AND TECHNIQUES

The Validate, Challenge, and Request Approach

A Practical Tool for Facilitating Difficult Dialogues

Kenneth V. Hardy, PhD

We believe that validation is a critical dimension of communication in all interpersonal interactions, and supervision is no exception. The act of *validating*, particularly within the context of interpersonal communication, is a means of extending legitimacy, corroboration, or validity to that which is expressed. With regards to conflictual communication, the act of validation provides a pathway for conversants and "combatants" alike to find common ground. In our view, validation is a crucial skill for supervisors to master and for supervisees to learn. The supervisor's use of validation allows for greater adherence to a Multicultural Relational Perspective (MRP) by adopting (a) a strengths-based approach to trainees' growth and development and (b) supporting a Both/And perspective.

THE VCR APPROACH

The VCR Approach is a strengths-based tool designed to facilitate difficult dialogues, especially those associated with Context Talk. The Approach is adaptable and can be used in virtually any situation, translating the core principles of healthy communication into interactions threatened by escalating conflict and rigid stand-offs. The VCR Approach is both a worldview and communication strategy (Hardy & Laszloffy, 2005). As a worldview it is predicated on the belief that "good and bad" are contained in the same shell and that there is something potentially redeemable and worthy contained even within the most egregious and outlandish behavior. The VCR as a worldview asserts that we tend to see what we look for, thus the seeking of pathology, for example, renders the finding of the same. Sometimes a shift in what we ultimately look for can substantially alter what we see. The strategy domain of the VCR trains the eye to search for the "redeemable" contained within a given behavior or interaction prior to searching for or focusing on the reprehensible. The VCR Approach comprises the following three steps:

1. "**V**" represents **Validation**, which refers to any communication (both verbal and non-verbal) designed to affirm. The validation step consists of the speaker sending a clear, strong message that conveys some understanding of the listener's point of view. The speaker must also express recognition of and respect for the listener's

strengths and positive qualities. An effective act of Validation highlights the redeemable aspect of either a person's being or an important component of the message that she or he has expressed.

2. "**C**" represents **Challenge**, which refers to any communication designed to question or confront. By validating, the listener builds a developing trust that makes it possible to follow with a challenging message. To be effective, it is crucial that the challenge follows the validation and that it does not assault the humanity or dignity of the listener. In fact, the most effective challenges weave in and build upon the earlier messages of validation.

3. "**R**" represents **Request,** which refers to an expressed desire for reconsideration of a position, and ultimately a specific recommendation or suggestion for change. After validating and challenging the listener, the final step is to make a request. Here is where the greatest corrective opportunity exists. The speaker makes a positive, concrete suggestion for how the listener can translate the stated concern into direct action for change.

While quite simple in its design, the VCR Approach is more than a technique as noted earlier. It is grounded in a way of thinking about the world and relationships. As such, the perceived simplicity of it can, at times, be deceptive. Moreover, even when one embraces the philosophy that underpins the VCR, coaching and repeated opportunities to practice it often are necessary before using it consistently and effectively.

Guiding Principles

The VCR Approach is grounded in several guiding principles. These principles form the philosophical framework for the VCR Approach.

Embrace Both/And Thinking

The embrace of Both/And thinking (Hardy, 1995) involves demonstrating the ability to see how two seemingly disparate entities can and often do co-exist. It reflects an acute appreciation for how entities that might first appear dichotomous, e.g., "good and bad," are actually contained in one another. With regards to the VCR Approach, embracing Both/And thinking is essential. It allows those in an intense relational encounter to appreciate how a given interaction or exchange that appears wholly *negative* and/or *offensive* can also contain an element that is *positive* and *potentially embracing*.

Validation Is the Key and Must Precede All Other Exchanges

Validation must always precede challenging especially during Context Talk where emotions tend to be volatile and the potential for feeling offended is heightened. When challenges, criticism, or confrontation occurs before there has been sufficient validation, the listener becomes defensive and tends to either withdraw from the interaction or assume an attacking stance. "Challenges" that precede validation limit the potential for any further constructive engagement and are hence, conversation blockers. Rather than conveying a commitment to the developing conversation and the relationship, the interaction becomes a competition regarding whose point-counterpoint is right. Unfortunately, the interaction is often usurped by the indignant rigidity of the "righteous rightness" of each party's respective position.

The Recipient Determines How Much Validation Is Needed

For the beginning users of the VCR, there is always the question regarding "How much validation is enough? How do you know when you have validated enough so that you can move onto challenging?" Once a facility with the approach is developed the question becomes easier to reconcile. It is the recipient of the validation, not the dispenser who determines when *she or he* has been validated adequately. To assess whether the recipient has been validated enough, the dispenser should pay close attention to the subtle cues that arise during communication. For example, if the recipient either overtly rejects the validation or if the recipient fails to signal some acceptance of the affirmation, either verbally or non-verbally, then more validation is needed. When the level of validation becomes sufficient, the recipient will begin to send cues that it is being embraced. For example, the recipient may start to nod her head affirmatively, or offer overt verbal affirmations ("Yes, you're right" or "You really understand") that indicate some acceptance of the validation. Each individual and each situation is unique. In some instances, a recipient may only require a few validating comments. In other cases, the dispenser may need to offer validation more liberally. The most compelling cue that additional validation is necessary is usually expressed by the degree of stagnation present in the interaction. If the conversation appears stuck, rehashing the same content, this is often a very strong indication that more effective validation is required.

The Degree of Validation Must Match the Intensity of the Affect

It is of paramount significance that the extent to which the dispenser offers validation is commensurate with the intensity of the emotion that the recipient is displaying. For example, in situations where the recipient is experiencing a minor level of distress, only a minor level of validation is likely to be needed. In situations where the recipient is expressing extreme distress, and/or has been subjected to severe devaluation, deeper, more sustained validation will be required.

The level of validation that is needed is often positively correlated with experiences with trauma or abuse, and/or with one's membership in a socially devalued group.

Experiences with trauma, abuse, and oppression are inherently devaluing. Those who have endured such experiences are likely to suffer from high dosages of devaluation, and will therefore require additional dosages of validation. Put another way, the best treatment for devaluation is validation.

The VCR Approach Expands Rather than Reduces

The VCR Approach is a strengths-based approach based on the principle of constructive expansion of relational possibilities rather than reduction, constriction, or suppression. The goal is not to validate *instead* of challenge, or to do more of one than the other, but rather to expand one's commentary enough to incorporate and balance both. The implicit invitation that the VCR Approach issues to its participants is to consider the possible ways in which one's standard way of participating in an interaction might be expanded to broaden the scope of untapped possibilities that may exist within the relationship (or interaction).

TIPS FOR EFFECTIVE EXECUTION

The VCR Approach is deceptively simple in design, but often difficult to execute. To facilitate use of the VCR Approach, there are several tips that are highly recommended. Users of the VCR, and those who are endeavoring to help others use it, should keep these pointers in mind at all times.

Avoid Asking Questions

It is critical to avoid asking questions when using the VCR Approach because questions are often hidden challenges. Consider an exchange that occurred between two participants in a workshop I was conducting. Portia, a middle-aged African American woman, was commenting on the distress that she and many Parents of Color have been experiencing regarding the alarming rate of unarmed young men of color killed by policemen. She stated tearfully, self-reflectively, and rhetorically: "We are a profession that has a name for every possible human condition that exists but we seem to have no name for the pain that mothers like me feel on a daily basis—what name do we assign to this type of racially-inflicted pain?" A White middle-aged woman attendee, Pam, who was obviously perturbed by Portia's comment retorted: "Are you also concerned about and looking for a name for all the black people that kill each other?"

While this appears on the surface to be a question, in fact it is a statement that is thinly veiled within a quasi-question. In my opinion, Pam was not seeking information. Instead she was making an "indirect" statement. Her question was clearly a poorly disguised challenge. Because questions can too easily become challenges in disguises, we strongly recommend avoiding questions altogether and instead making clear, direct statements. Her question was legitimate but the timing and the absence of validation were problematic.

Connect the V, C, and R

It is crucial that the V, C, and R are all interrelated in a coherent and meaningful way. After the validation has been dispensed, the challenge needs to build upon it, and the request should then follow from these. When this type of connectedness is missing, the major objective of the VCR is lost altogether. If it is too much validation void of the challenge and request, the interaction sputters from a perceived lack of authenticity. When the Challenge is out of sync with the Validation and Request, it adds an element of aggression and an abusive-like dynamic that is exceedingly counterproductive. And finally, if the message is greatly skewed towards the Request message to the exclusion of corresponding Validation and Challenge messages, it often makes for a very superficial low-intensity relationship with "harmonious" but insincere outcomes.

Replace the Term "But" with "And"

The purpose that "but" serves is to erase or negate all that comes before it. Hence, when "but" follows validation, it undermines the validation by canceling it out altogether. For this reason it is recommended that the word "but" is replaced with the word "and." Unlike "but," the term "and" is expansive. When "and" is used it means "in addition to." Therefore, when "and" follows validation, it means that, "in addition to these factors, please also consider these other issues."

Recognize the Relationship between Power and Responsibility

With power comes responsibility. The person possessing the greatest power and privilege in the relationship relative to a given conversation has the responsibility to initiate and sustain the Validation process. For example, in supervision, supervisors have the responsibility to initiate the VCR Approach because they have greater power in the relationship. The same holds true for the therapy relationship as well. It is the responsibility of the therapist to validate even when standing in the pathway of extreme negative feedback from a client.

POTENTIAL PITFALLS

There are several pitfalls that can complicate and undermine the effective use of the VCR Approach. Several of the most common pitfalls are discussed below.

Confusing Validation with Agreement

The failure to distinguish between Validation and agreement is one of the greatest challenges to executing the VCR effectively. These are two distinct concepts and should not be confused, yet they often are. Validation conveys understanding but also, more importantly, an appreciation for the attribute that is embedded in either the message conveyed or exhibited by the speaker. It is possible to understand something and express appreciation without necessarily agreeing with it. Agreement, on the other hand, connotes reaching a point of concurrence. Validation does not condone or suggest agreement with a particular position or perspective. For example, referring back to the workshop attendee, Pam, who was mentioned earlier, rather than responding with a challenge disguised as a question she could have alternatively stated: "I really appreciate the sense of passionate connection you feel towards the mothers you are working with." A comment such as this would not have been tantamount to an endorsement of Portia's statement. Instead, it was merely a validation of a potential redeemable aspect Pam could see embedded in Portia's emotional disclosure. The Validation would not have deterred Pam from overtly expressing any disagreement that she might have had with Portia's statement.

Orientation toward Punishment or Revenge

Adopting an orientation towards punishment and revenge can be common reactions to experiencing feelings of hurt, disappointment, and criticism. The tendency to quickly push back, counter-attack, or to resort to punitive and vengeful actions make the VCR virtually impossible to effectively implement. The impulsive inclination to respond aggressively or punitively to someone prior to Validating should be averted.

Discomfort with the Intimacy of Validating

Discomfort with expressing the intimacy that is embedded in validation is another impediment to utilizing the VCR Approach effectively. To offer another validation is to build a connection with that other person (or group). Validation brings people closer, it depolarizes relationships, it neutralizes negativity, and it bridges distances and establishes alliances. This can be particularly disconcerting depending upon the person and situation within which one is attempting to offer validation. For example, when speaking to someone who has committed an act of aggression, it is difficult to imagine offering validation and hence moving closer to this person. For many of us, our instinct is to want to distance ourselves from someone who has acted aggressively, not to build closeness with that person. Hence, in situations where one experiences some fear or repulsion toward the person to whom one should be offering validation, doing so can be extremely difficult.

When the "V" is Delivered Lacking Authenticity

It is extremely important that when a Validating message is given, it is done with sincerity and authenticity. It is quite easy to differentiate between a "V" that is authentic versus one that is merely perfunctory. One of the things that undermine the sincerity of a "V" message is when the dispenser is too eager to move onto the "C." In such instances, they extend the "V" only as a matter of task, and not because they genuinely believe in what they are saying. These types of "V" messages almost always fail miserably. It is vital for the dispenser to look within and find something genuine that she or he can validate and to take the time to offer this validation in a heartfelt and authentic manner.

Associating Challenging with Being Attacking, Abrasive, or Judgmental

While validating can be difficult to do in certain situations and under certain circumstances, there are situations within which it also can be hard to Challenge. Especially for those who were raised in families that were highly conflict-avoidant or highly conflictual, the idea of Challenging can be threatening. There may be a tendency to associate all Challenging with a form of attacking, abrasiveness, or judgmentalism. While it is possible for Challenges to be presented in ways that embody all of these attributes, the most effective ones are those that do not assault, condemn, or denigrate. In fact, the most artful Challenges build upon the previous validation and culminate in inviting the recipient to consider something from a new perspective.

Tendency to Split the V, C, and R

It is imperative that all three steps of the VCR are executed, and that this occurs in sequence. It is very tempting to want to begin with Challenging and then move to Validation, but it is essential that Validation come first. It also is common to effectively execute the "V" and the "C" but to not culminate in offering the "R." The overall effectiveness of the Approach is predicated on the interactional interplay that exists between and among the V, the C, and the R.

The VCR Approach can be a very effective tool for effectively engaging in Context Talk and avoiding stuck and deeply entrenched non-progressive conversations. When used liberally and effectively it is a potent lubricant for stagnant and repetitively stuck relationships and communication patterns.

REFERENCES

Hardy, K. V. (1995). Embracing Both/And. *Psychotherapy Networker, 19*(6), 42–57.

Hardy, K. V., & Laszloffy, T. A. (2005). *Teens Who Hurt: Clinical Interventions for Breaking the Cycle of Adolescent Violence.* New York, NY: Guilford Press.

7

Essential Skills for Mastering Context Talk in Supervision

Kenneth V. Hardy, PhD

Context Talk refers to any conversation or dialogue that involves a dimension of diversity. Whether in the classroom, consulting room, or in supervision, the task of effectively and seamlessly integrating Context Talk into the process is often a challenging endeavor even for the most experienced Supervisor and/or Trainer. Most attempts to talk openly and candidly about virtually any dimension of diversity are frequently greeted with extreme caution and trepidation, unabashed avoidance, or conflict escalation. In any case, the results are usually the same: an absence of meaningful engagement involving Context Talk. The more Context Talk is avoided, the more difficult it is to develop the experience, comfort, and skill to have meaningful conversations. One of the principal reasons underlying the hesitancy or unwillingness to fully engage in Context Talk is the lack of "know how" or skill to do so. Like any other challenging topic, Context Talk requires possession of a well-honed skill set to ensure its relative success. Full and effective engagement in Context Talk requires participants to have some degree of mastery of both basic communication skills as well as a keen understanding of advanced Context Talk-related skills. Both are briefly highlighted below.

BASIC COMMUNICATION SKILLS

Basic communication skills comprise those strategies that are germane to the execution of effective interpersonal communication regardless of topic or participants. Many of these skills are considered fundamental to the training of clinicians and are often a staple in training and supervisory processes. The following list of basic communication skills is composed of those that are considered to be most salient to providing a solid foundation for effectively engaging in Context Talk.

1. **Deep Listening**—This critical skill involves listening with a purpose. At its core it involves being completely devoted to listening to and understanding the disclosure of a speaker. It requires the Deep Listener to suspend one's personal inclinations to interrupt, being distracted by the formulation of one's rebuttal or retort, and to be

fully committed to understanding another's point of view. Deep Listening also involves listening with a "third ear," which focuses not only listening to *words and content* but also attending to or being curious about *the meaning* attached to words and content.

2. **Providing Skillful Feedback**—Feedback is skillful when it conveys to the Speaker that their message has been received openly and non-defensively. It is expressed in a way that takes into account the needs of both the Speaker and the (Deep) Listener.

3. **Using "I Messages"**—"I messages" are crucial to effective interpersonal communication for three main reasons: 1) they situate the Speakers into the conversation; 2) they enable the Speaker to assume accountability for one's thoughts and feelings; and 3) they avoid the usage of "You Messages" which tends to affix blame.

4. **Attending to Verbal and Non-Verbal Communication**—So much of what gets communicated interpersonally is often done so without the benefit of a spoken word. Thus, being attuned to and adept at recognizing both verbal and non-verbal communication is essential to effective communication. Facial expressions, shifts in body positioning, exaggerated kinetic activity, just to cite a few, are all frequently potent forms of communication.

5. **Developing Refined Meta-Communication Skills**—Communicating about communication is the nucleus of meta-communication. When efforts to communicate invariably break down or get stuck, having the ability to shift from the "stuck conversation" to a "conversation about the 'stuckness' of the communication" is often the perfect antidote to stagnant interaction.

6. **Developing a Communication Style that Imbues Intimacy, Intensity, Congruency, Authenticity, and Transparency**—The overall quality of effective interpersonal communication is significantly affected by the skillful implementation of these five, highly intertwined, principal factors of communication. *Intimacy* refers to the ability to be emotionally open in one's approach to communication. It doesn't require one to be emotionally expressive necessarily but it doesn't preclude it either. For example, merely stating: "I am sorry, I made a mistake" can be a very intimate disclosure to make in a conversation. *Intensity* ultimately involves developing "the muscle" to cope with discomfort. It can often be measured by the willingness one exhibits to take conversational risks—to stretch beyond one's normal zone of comfort. The absence of intensity often threatens *Congruency*, which is the level of consonance that exists between one's words and actions, and/or expressed thoughts and feelings. *Authenticity* is an important mechanism by which congruency can be solidified. Authenticity is the ability to honestly and openly *say what you mean and mean what you say*. When this is accomplished so is congruency. Transparency refers to the ability to show one's "authentic self" as well as the willingness to have it seen by others.

7. **Effectively Using Expressions of Acknowledgment**—Demonstrating the ability to express acknowledgement is an important feature of providing skillful feedback. Expressions of acknowledgment convey to a Speaker that their message has been received and embraced even in the face of disagreement. It is an overt recognition that a message has been received.

8. **Responding Therapeutically**—Any form of communication that thwarts an interaction designed to escalate constitutes a therapeutic response. For example, using expressions of acknowledgement can be extremely effective in de-escalating interactions that are headed towards escalation.

9. **Develop Proficiency in Expressing Thoughts and Feeling**—Effective communication requires overt expressions of thoughts and feelings. The expression of thoughts and feelings is necessary to communicate with intimacy, intensity, congruency, authenticity, and transparency.

10. **Create Space for Silence, Reflection, and Contemplation**—Developing comfort with extended periods of silence (intensity) in conversations helps to create space for reflection and contemplation. It affords participants in a conversation the opportunity to be more thoughtful and less prone to making random and impulsive comments.

In addition to refining the aforementioned basic skills, mastering Context Talk also requires having a working knowledge of and facility with the execution of the following advanced skills.

ADVANCED SKILLS

1. **Develop a Multidimensional View of the Self**—The development of this conceptual skill involves having the ability to see one's self culturally. In so doing there is a keen awareness that one's self comprises a number of contextual variables, including but not limited to, ethnicity, religion, class, ability, etc.

2. **Know Thy Selves**—Following the development of a *Multidimensional View of the Self*, it is crucial to become acquainted with all of our (contextual) selves. Moreover, it is important to become intimately familiar with and acutely aware of the dimensions of one's self that are privileged (i.e., valued in the larger society) and those that are subjugated (i.e., devalued in the broader society).

3. **Location of a Self**—An integral part of knowing thyself involves knowing which dimension of one's self is implicated in a specific version of Context Talk. For instance, if the Context Talk is centered on religion, then it becomes imperative that one's "religious self" is located in the conversation. To introduce any other dimension of one's self to a conversation about religion would be a breach of appropriately locating one's self as well as tantamount to shifting the focus of the conversation from religion to another dimension.

4. **Perform the Tasks of the Privileged and/or the Tasks of the Subjugated when Appropriate**—During Context Talk, the person or group with the greatest power and privilege in the relationship must assume greater responsibility for navigating the interaction. Context Talk generally progresses more smoothly when those in the Privileged Position exercise the Tasks of the Privileged and those in the Subjugated Position can implement the Tasks of the Subjugated.

Two critical tasks of the Privileged are: 1) Resist the Equalization of Suffering; and 2) Address the *consequences* of one's diversity-related transgressions and micro-aggressions rather than clarifying the purity of one's good intentions.

The *Equalization of Suffering* occurs when the Privileged attempts to reassure the Subjugated that there is no difference in their respective "pain." While there is no way to determine whose pain is more severe, the significant point here is the failure of the Privileged to authentically acknowledge and validate what is considered by the Subjugated to be their unique painful experience. The failure to resist the Equalization of Suffering has dire consequences for the effective execution of Context Talk.

Addressing the consequences of one's actions, rather than focusing on one's good intentions is the other major Task of the Privileged. When the Privileged engages in clarifying and re-stating one's honorable intentions, it unwittingly shifts a conversation away from *how* the Subjugated has been hurt, slighted, offended, etc. (consequence) to the declaration that the hurt was unintended (intentions). Context Talk that privileges the intentions of the Privileged becomes a *privileged conversation* that inevitably stifles the process. It abdicates the Privileged of any accountability to the Subjugated while simultaneously dismissing the significance of the disclosure by the latter.

Two critical tasks of the Subjugated are: 1) Overcoming Learned Voiceless-ness and 2) Refraining from Care-taking of the Privileged. Just as the Privileged must perform the Tasks of the Privileged, the Subjugated must also carry out the tasks associated with its position.

Overcoming Learned Voicelessness is one of the most vital tasks to be performed by the Subjugated. After all, meaningful Context Talk is virtually impossible without the active participation of the Subjugated. Overcoming learned voicelessness requires the Subjugated to become self-advocates. It highlights the significance and utter necessity of the Subjugated naming, claiming, and vocalizing their thoughts, feelings, and experiences to and in the presence of the Privileged. In accomplishing this feat, the Subjugated also exercises the related and assigned task of *Refraining from Care-Taking of the Privileged*.

The Subjugated is socialized to emotionally, and in some instances, physically take care of the Privileged. The Care-Taking of the Privileged is usually accomplished by assuming actions and behaviors that are ultimately designed to ensure the comfort of the Privileged. Typical care-taking maneuvers often include remaining silent when one has to speak, denying one's feelings, thoughts, and existence in the face of the Privileged, hyper-compliant behavior, as well as a host of other self-deprecating gestures and behaviors. While all of these behaviors are exceedingly successful in maintaining "peaceful, non-conflictual" interactions on the surface, they are ultimately counterproductive to engaging in effective Context Talk or building relationships across differences.

5. **Use the VCR Approach Efficiently**—Effective use of the VCR approach requires those in communication and dialogue to refine their skills regarding Validating, Challenging, and Requesting. It also promotes Both/And thinking, where seemingly disparate ideas can co-exist. Validation is not only a form of acknowledgement (as discussed earlier) but is also a tool of affirmation. It requires a Listener, for example, to recognize and affirm redeemable aspects of a Speaker, even when his or her message has been attacking, destructive, or unsavory in some other way. Whereas the **V**alidation would address the redeemable aspect of the Speaker, the **C**hallenge would focus on the part of the message that was problematic. Thus a message could consist of properties that were **both** worthy of validation **and** a challenge simultaneously. The request is a verbal invitation for the Speaker to maintain and solidify the redeemable part while also refining or altering the non-functional part of a message.

> The following is an example of a Supervisor's use of the VCR with an angry supervisee:
>
> **Validation**: "Jeff I really appreciate your willingness to openly and authentically engage with me in a conversation about your experiences with Black people."
>
> **Challenge**: "**AND** at the same time I found myself distracted … almost paralyzed by your repeated use of the *N* word."
>
> **Request**: "I am hoping that you will continue to remain open to having authentic conversations about race and your experience with Black people **and** that you can do it in a way that doesn't rely on your usage of hurtful racial epithets. Would you be willing to keep these important conversations going without the racial epithets?"

Engaging effectively in Context Talk and smoothly integrating it into training and supervision requires considerable preparation. The adroit usage of well-integrated basic and advanced communication skills is critical to initiating, conducting, and maintaining effective Context Talk especially when meaningful and progressive outcomes are the goal.

8

The Cultural Genogram

Key to Training Culturally Competent Family Therapists

Kenneth V. Hardy, PhD and Tracey A. Laszloffy, PhD

This chapter has been reprinted (with permission from the Journal of Marital and Family Therapy) *from an article (1995, Vol. 21, No. 3, 227–237) by Kenneth V. Hardy, PhD and Tracey A. Laszloffy, PhD.[1] Training programs committed to the development of culturally competent family therapists must discover ways to raise cultural awareness and increase cultural sensitivity. While awareness involves gaining knowledge of various cultural groups, sensitivity involves having experiences that challenge individuals to explore their personal cultural issues. This chapter outlines how the cultural genogram can be used as an effective training tool to promote both cultural awareness and sensitivity.*

To meet the demands of a changing world, it will be imperative for family therapy training programs to devote greater attention to preparing culturally competent therapists. Unfortunately, current efforts to prepare culturally competent therapists are skewed heavily toward promoting cultural "awareness" while neglecting the importance of cultural "sensitivity." This occurs primarily through the use of multicultural training models that rely heavily on providing trainees with multicultural content, with far less emphasis upon promoting meaningful multicultural experiences.

Although it is beneficial for trainees to receive exposure to content highlighting the unique aspects of various cultural groups, it is rare that such knowledge readily translates into sensitivity. The content-focused approach to multicultural education overemphasizes the characteristics of various cultural groups while ignoring the importance of the trainees' perceptions of and feelings toward their respective cultural backgrounds. As a result, trainees are rarely challenged to examine how their respective cultural identities influence understanding and acceptance of those who are both culturally similar and dissimilar.

AWARENESS AND SENSITIVITY

Training programs devoted to preparing culturally competent therapists must recognize and attend to the distinction between awareness and sensitivity. Awareness is primarily a cognitive function; an individual becomes conscious of a thought or action and processes it intellectually. Sensitivity, on the other hand, is primarily an affective function; an individual responds emotionally to stimuli with delicacy and respectfulness. Although these functions appear unique and separate, each is shaded with nuances of the other. Essentially, awareness involves a conscious sensitivity, and sensitivity involves a delicate awareness.

Although most individuals possess varying degrees of awareness and sensitivity, training programs devoted to preparing culturally competent therapists must facilitate a greater interface between these functions. This article describes how the genogram can be used as a training tool to promote cultural awareness and sensitivity.

Human service professionals from a range of disciplines have cited various clinical applications of the genogram. It has been used to facilitate joining between client and therapist (Carter & Orfandis, 1976; Guerin & Pendagast, 1976; Pendagast & Sherman, 1977) and to gain insight into the client's psyche (Watchel, 1982). Family practitioners have used it as a data-gathering device (Doherty & Baird, 1983; Jolly, Froom, & Rosen, 1980; Milhorn, 1981; Rogers & Durkin, 1984; Sproul & Gallagher, 1982), and family therapists have used it as an assessment tool (Hartman, 1977; Kramer, 1985; McGoldrick & Gerson, 1985).

THE CULTURAL GENOGRAM

The primary goal of the cultural genogram is to promote cultural awareness and sensitivity by helping trainees to understand their cultural identities. Through this process, trainees gain greater insight into and appreciation for the ways in which culture impacts their role as therapists and influences the lives of clients in treatment. The cultural genogram is designed to accomplish its primary goal by (a) illustrating and clarifying the influence that culture has on the family system; (b) assisting trainees in identifying the groups which contribute to the formation of their cultural identity; (c) encouraging candid discussions that reveal and challenge culturally-based assumptions and stereotypes; (d) assisting trainees in discovering their culturally-based emotional triggers (i.e., unresolved culturally-based conflicts); and (e) assisting trainees in exploring how their unique cultural identities may impact their therapeutic style and effectiveness.

CULTURE AND ETHNICITY

One of the major conceptual challenges associated with completing a cultural genogram involves understanding the relationship between "culture" and "ethnicity." There is widespread confusion regarding the relationship between these two concepts. Within the family therapy literature, for example, some authors consider culture to be more expansive than ethnicity (Falicov, 1988) while others use them synonymously (McGoldrick, 1985; Preli & Bernard, 1993).

Figure 8.1 The Cultural Genogram

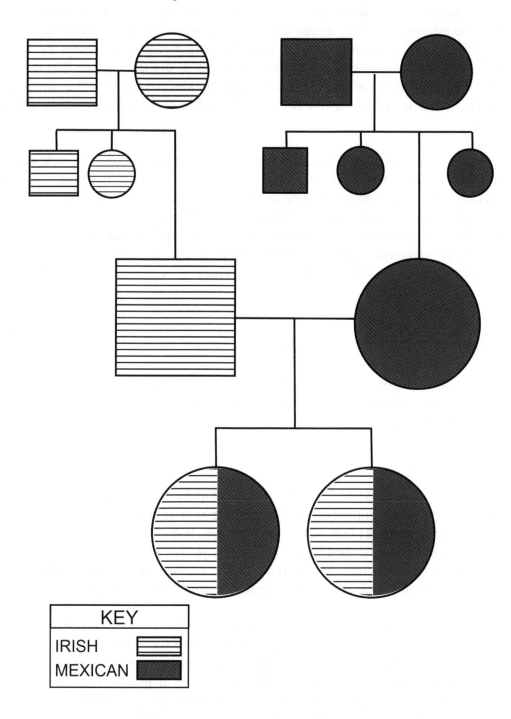

Although not reflected in the family therapy literature, the genogram also has been used widely as a training tool. Bahr (1990) explains that as a training tool, the objective of the genogram is to help both illustrate and clarify family systems concepts and to help trainees get in touch with their personal emotional family-of-origin issues. Using the genogram for training differs from using it as a clinical tool. As a training tool, "the objective is to help students visualize and understand their family system and their own place within it, rather than to change it" (Bahr, 1990, p. 243).

The cultural genogram is based on the assumption that culture and ethnicity are both interrelated and distinct. Culture is a broad multidimensional concept that includes but is not limited to ethnicity, gender, social class, and so forth. Ethnicity, on the other hand, refers to the group(s) from which an individual has descended and derives the essence of her/his sense of "peoplehood." Therefore, when all of the dimensions that contribute to culture converge (e.g., ethnicity, social class, gender), they form the whole of an individual's cultural identity. It is this whole in which the cultural genogram is ultimately interested.

Culture represents the principal focus of the cultural genogram; however, ethnicity is an integral part of the process and serves as a primary vehicle for promoting understanding of one's cultural identity. Using ethnicity as a means toward understanding culture is an approach used commonly by other educators and trainers of cultural diversity. For instance, Falicov (1988) notes that "one way for trainees to learn to think *culturally* [italics added] is for them to interview a non-clinical family of a distinct *ethnic* [italics added] or socioeconomic group" (p. 339). Thus, ethnicity constitutes a means to an end rather than *the* end.

PREPARING A CULTURAL GENOGRAM

Preparing a cultural genogram requires careful thought and planning. The following section outlines the steps necessary for constructing and presenting a comprehensive cultural genogram.

Getting Organized

Defining one's culture of origin. The first critical step in preparing a cultural genogram involves defining one's culture of origin. For the purposes of this exercise, culture of origin refers to the major group(s) from which an individual has descended that were the first generation to come to the United States (except for Native Americans). For example, an individual may have been born and raised in America, but if her/his grandparents were Irish and Greek, then the culture of origin consists of these two groups.

Organizing principles and pride/shame issues. The next step in preparing a cultural genogram is identifying the major organizing principles of each group that comprises the trainee's culture of origin. Organizing principles are fundamental constructs which shape the perceptions, beliefs, and behaviors of members of a group. They are the basic structures upon which all other aspects of a culture are predicated. Identifying organizing principles serves to establish a framework, which is an essential step in organizing and constructing an effective cultural genogram presentation.

Trainees also should identify pride/shame issues for each group associated with their culture of origin. Pride/shame issues are aspects of a culture that are sanctioned as distinctively negative or positive. They derive their meaning from organizing principles. Understanding the distinction between organizing principles and pride/shame issues is important. They are similar in that both organize the perceptions, beliefs, and behaviors of group members.

However, the critical distinction between the two is that pride/shame issues punctuate behaviors as negative or positive, while organizing principles do not. For instance, in Jewish culture, fear of persecution is an organizing principle, and educational achievement is a pride/shame issue. Although both of these organize Jewish people, educational achievement, unlike fear of persecution, punctuates the individual behavior of Jews as either positive or negative.

Identifying organizing principles and pride/shame issues requires trainees to utilize a variety of sources. These sources may include drawing from one's personal knowledge of a group, conducting interviews with members from a particular group, or reviewing reference materials, such as films, books, or cultural artifacts.

Creating symbols. Symbols should be designed by the trainee to denote all pride/shame issues. They should be placed directly on the cultural genogram to depict graphically the prevalence of pride/shame issues and to highlight their impact on family functioning. The use of symbols is a form of analogic communication that allows the presenter to express the intuitive and affective aspects of cultural issues that are sometimes difficult to capture with words. Essentially, using symbols provides trainees with a means for communicating the nonrational, emotional dimensions of cultural issues that often defy verbal expression.

Selecting colors. A different color should be selected to represent each group comprising a trainee's culture of origin. The colors are used to identify different groups and to depict how each group contributes to the cultural identity of each individual. For instance, if a female is half Swedish (yellow), a quarter Ugandan (red), and a quarter Venezuelan (blue), then the circle that identifies her on the genogram would be color-coded half yellow, a quarter red, and a quarter blue.

The configuration of colors provides a graphic snapshot of the overall cultural composition of the family system and of each individual's unique cultural identity. The initial "color snapshot" inspires a variety of initial hypotheses about the family system and the trainee. For instance, genograms that are dominated by a single color reveal that the family system is characterized by a high degree of cultural homogeneity. On the other hand, genograms that are a collage of colors quickly reveal the multiculturalism of the family system. From these initial observations, numerous questions can be generated to guide further exploration, interpretation, and understanding of the trainees' unique cultural issues and identities.

Identifying intercultural marriages. Intercultural marriages represent a blending of cultures and hence a blending of organizing principles and pride/shame issues. Cultural differences in marriage often have a significant influence on the nature of the relationship and on children. Therefore, in addition to identifying where intercultural marriages occur, trainees should also (a) explore how divergent cultural issues were/are negotiated and (b) trace the intergenerational consequences of the intercultural union. Trainees should use the (~) symbol to denote intercultural marriages.

Putting it Together

Cultural framework charts. Establishing cultural framework charts (CFC) is the next crucial step in the cultural genogram process. The CFC is to the cultural genogram as a legend is to a map. In other words, it provides the keys for interpreting the genogram. A CFC is necessary for each group comprising one's culture of origin. It should list the major organizing principles and the pride/shame issues with their corresponding symbols.

Genogram. The final preparatory step involves constructing at least a three-generation family genogram and adding the following elements to it: the (~) symbol to identify intercultural marriages, colors to illustrate the cultural composition of each person's cultural identity, and the symbols denoting pride/shame issues.

Questions to consider. It is also recommended that trainees answer the questions outlined in Table 8.1: "Questions to Consider While Preparing for the Cultural Genogram Presentation." Trainees' familiarity with the answers to these questions can facilitate an informed dialogue about the various sociological factors (e.g., race, religion, regionality, class) that contribute to cultural identity. Through addressing these questions they will be encouraged to appreciate the complexity of cultural identity formation.

INTERPRETATION AND PRESENTATION

The cultural genogram presentation should begin with an introduction of the trainee's cultural framework chart(s). This portion of the process is primarily didactic. Trainees introduce, and discuss in detail, organizing principles, pride/shame issues, and the colors and symbols they have selected.

After presenting the cultural framework chart(s), the next step involves using the genogram as a means to illustrate the issues delineated in the chart(s). Essentially, trainees use their genograms to identify and trace the presence or absence of the various pride/shame issues defined on their chart(s). It is recommended that trainees begin exploring the transmission of cultural issues from the oldest generation on their genogram through the subsequent generations. This portion of the process is primarily experiential and involves considerable interaction and discussion.

Synthesis

The cultural genogram experience should culminate in an analysis of a trainee's cultural background, highlighting how it shapes her/his cultural identity and impacts her/his role as a therapist. The synthesis stage enables trainees to reflect upon, further explore, and integrate the various aspects of the entire process. It is during this stage that trainees are encouraged to think critically about themselves as cultural beings. They should be challenged to describe and analyze at least one critical incident from each stage of the cultural genogram process (i.e., "Getting Organized," "Putting It All Together," etc.).

Table 8.1 Questions to Consider while Preparing for the Cultural Genogram
Presentation

Please consider these questions for each group constituting your culture of origin, as well as considering the implications of the answers in relation to your overall cultural identity.

1. What were the migration patterns of the group?

2. If other than Native American, under what conditions did your family (or their descendants) enter the United States (immigrant, political refugee, slave, etc.)?

3. What were/are the group's experiences with oppression? What were/are the markers of oppression?

4. What issues divide members within the same group? What are the sources of intragroup conflict?

5. Describe the relationship between the group's identity and your national ancestry (if the group is defined in terms of nationality, please skip this question).

6. What significance does race, skin color, and hair play within the group?

7. What is/are the dominant religion(s) of the group? What role does religion and spirituality play in the everyday lives of members of the group?

8. What role does regionality and geography play in the group?

9. How are gender roles defined within the group? How is sexual orientation regarded?

10. a)   What prejudices or stereotypes does this group have about itself?

    b)   What prejudices and stereotypes do other groups have about this group?

    c)   What prejudices or stereotypes does this group have about other groups?

11. What role (if any) do names play in the group? Are there rules, mores, or rituals governing the assignment of names?

12. How is social class defined in the group?

13. What occupational roles are valued and devalued by the group?

14. What is the relationship between age and the values of the group?

15. How is family defined in the group?

16. How does this group view outsiders in general and mental health professionals specifically?

17. How have the organizing principles of this group shaped your family and its members? What effect have they had on you?

18. What are the ways in which pride/shame issues of each group are manifested in your family system?

19. What impact will these pride/shame issues have on your work with clients from both similar and dissimilar cultural backgrounds?

20. If your culture of origin comprises more than one group, how were the differences negotiated in your family? What were the intergenerational consequences? How has this impacted you personally and as a therapist?

There are two basic tasks associated with this stage. The first is retrospective self-reflection, which encourages trainees to ponder the impact of the cultural genogram process ex post facto. The central question germane to successful completion of this task is "now that it's over, what did I learn from it?" The second task is integration, which involves inspiring trainees to search for the goodness of fit between thoughts and feelings, content and process, and their personal and professional identities, as each of these has been shaped by the cultural genogram process. It is through completion of these interrelated tasks that trainees incorporate what they have gained from the exercise into their clinical work.

The synthesis process occurs over an extended period of time. However, it may be necessary and even desirable for trainers to establish artificial benchmarks to represent a point of closure for the cultural genogram process. Thus, the synthesis stage, as described here, is a ritual that symbolizes an end to the cultural genogram process and the beginning of an ongoing process of cultural self-exploration and integration.

The Role of the Facilitator

The facilitator assumes a crucial role in the overall success of the cultural genogram experience. It is necessary for the facilitator to support the trainees emotionally during this self-exploratory process while remaining detached enough to challenge them intellectually. As with any experience of this type, successful execution of the facilitator's role is largely dependent on the extent to which her/his emotional involvement in the overall process is managed effectively. It is only through achieving an appropriate balance between engagement and disengagement that the facilitator can create the emotional climate necessary to stimulate emotional sharing and intellectual exploration.

An effective facilitator (a) clarifies the goals of the exercise and evaluates trainees' attainment of the goals; (b) determines what factors impeded or stimulated trainees' abilities to accomplish their goals; (c) demonstrates sensitivity to and respect for differences and the numerous ways in which differences are manifested, for example, how trainees learn and process information; (d) takes an active role in creating a milieu that promotes emotional safety and risk taking; (e) encourages trainees to challenge respectfully racial, ethnic, and ultimately cultural stereotypes and biases; and (f) demonstrates a tolerance for and an ability to manage escalating levels of anxiety, anger, and fear.

Because of the hypersensitivity that often characterizes cross-cultural interactions, it is important for the facilitator to remain comfortable with and even encourage interactions that often result in increased anxiety, fear, and frustration. The facilitator's overt display of comfort (or lack thereof) becomes either the catalyst for, or impediment to, heightened risk taking, meaningful sharing, and cultural sensitivity. Since trainees are often hesitant to discuss cultural differences openly for fear of "saying the wrong thing," the facilitator must assume the interrelated roles of interaction catalyst and broker of permission. It is primarily through these roles that trainees will be inspired and challenged to gain the essence of the cultural genogram process.

Table 8.2 Questions to Answer in Synthesis Paper

1. What are your family's beliefs and feelings about the group(s) that make up your culture of origin? What parts of the group(s) do they embrace or reject? How has this influenced your feelings about your cultural identity?

2. What aspects of your culture of origin do you have the most comfort "owning," the most difficulty "owning"?

3. What groups will you have the easiest time working with, the most difficult?

4. What did you learn about yourself and your cultural identity? How might this influence your tendencies as a therapist?

5. Was the exercise valuable, worthwhile? Why or why not?

Table 8.3 outlines sample questions facilitators might ask to help guide the cultural genogram presentations and related discussions.

Table 8.3 Questions for Facilitators to Consider During the Presentation

1. a) What does the content of the presentation teach about the presenter's culture of origin?

   b) What does the process of the presentation teach about the presenter's culture of origin?

   c) What parallels, if any, exist between the presenter's style and the cultural content disclosed?

2. Are family-of-origin and culture of-origin issues appropriately differentiated?

3. Do the colors and symbols chosen by the presenter have special cultural relevance? How were these chosen?

4. Is there a disproportionate number of pride or shame issues? What is the presenter's rationale for the schism?

5. When there are multiple groups comprising a trainee's culture of origin, how are they presented/negotiated?

6. How comfortable is the presenter in engaging in an open dialogue about inter- and/or intragroup prejudices and stereotypes?

7. What issues appear too uncomfortable for the presenter to discuss?

8. What impact did the presentation have on other trainees? What are the hypotheses regarding why such reactions were generated?

9. What relevance or insights did the presenter have as a result of this experience?

10. What was the process by which the information for the cultural genogram was gathered?

IMPLICATIONS FOR TREATMENT AND RESEARCH

Clinical Implications

Several family therapists (Hardy, 1990; Lappin, 1983) have emphasized the importance of therapists knowing their respective cultures before attempting to work cross-culturally. Lappin (1983) asserts that "knowing thy own culture is perhaps the most difficult aspect of conducting effective cross cultural therapy" (p. 135). To facilitate this process, Lappin recommends that the first step one must take is to develop a three-generational cultural genogram.

The cultural genogram not only helps therapists become more conversant with their cultural identities but also highlights culturally linked issues that may impede effective treatment. The didactic portion of the cultural genogram provides valuable contextual information about specific groups that can be beneficial in treatment. This is particularly true of groups with whom the therapist has had no previous contact. Rather than using the information as the basis for perpetuating stereotypes, it allows therapists to generate culturally-based hypotheses that can help shape the course of treatment.

The presentations and discussions associated with the cultural genogram are valuable and have strong implications for clinical practice. The exercise can be instrumental in assisting therapists to identify unresolved culturally-based issues. Resolution of these issues allows therapists to work more effectively cross-culturally, as well as with clients who are culturally similar.

Culturally unresolved therapists experience considerable difficulty demonstrating sensitivity to clients from similar and dissimilar backgrounds. For example, a therapist of Brazilian descent who rejects her/his heritage may find it difficult to work with Brazilian clients. This therapist may either express inappropriate affect toward any aspect of the client's background that appears unequivocally Brazilian, or efforts may be made to coerce the client indirectly to embrace her/his heritage more fully. In either case, it is the therapist's unresolved cultural issues that become a major organizing principle in treatment.

The cultural genogram experience also helps to shape the worldview of therapists. Rather than embracing the theoretical myth of sameness (the belief that all families are the same), therapists develop a genuine appreciation of and respect for the differences that exist between and among families. It is through this process therapists learn, for example, that there are some families for whom Saturday is not an appropriate day for therapy appointments or for whom it does make a difference whether they are thought of as Puerto Rican or Hispanic.

RESEARCH IMPLICATIONS

McGoldrick and Gerson (1985) and Lewis (1989) have emphasized the need for more empirical research on the genogram. The cultural genogram could benefit from empirical inquiry regarding its effectiveness. Outcome data gathered from training and clinical settings could enhance reliability and validity of the cultural genogram as an effective training tool for promoting culturally competent family therapists.

As family therapy programs continue to struggle with how to integrate multiculturalism into their curricula, data obtained from the cultural genogram could serve as a useful guide. The cultural genogram could be used as an instrument to collect aggregate data from training programs to highlight implications for how multiculturalism might (or might not) be incorporated into MFT curricula. Programs would have not only a wealth of rich trainee data to draw upon but also a variety of experiences with a myriad of teaching methodologies.

The cultural genogram, although conceived of as a training tool, may have some clinical applicability as well. Future research may determine that the instrument can be modified to use clinically in two significant ways: (a) as a basis for collecting/analyzing therapists' cultural competence in cross-cultural family therapy and (b) as an assessment instrument in working with cross-cultural families where the blending of cultural issues is the presenting problem or related to it.

The need and implications for further research are enormous. Questions regarding the specifics of such research should remain part of an open and continuing dialogue.

REFLECTIONS ON THE CULTURAL GENOGRAM

The cultural genogram is a practical instrument for assisting trainees in becoming more familiar with their culturally constructed realities. The process of developing, using, and refining the instrument has assisted the authors in this goal as well. The cultural genogram has been instrumental in heightening our awareness of our cultural biases and the numerous ways in which these are deeply embedded in the cultural genogram process. Thus, we wish to admonish trainers and trainees that the instrument and recommended process are only as objective as our cultural lenses would permit us to be. Everything we have described, recommended, or chosen to include or ignore has been "tarnished" by our Westernized view of the world.

For example, a Hindu trainee from Southern India pointed out the cultural bias ingrained in our assumption that a complete family system can be mapped out in a single two-dimensional diagram. She explained that in her culture, the definition of family is much more expansive than in Western society. In constructing her cultural genogram, she was forced by the limitations of the standardized genogram format to leave out many individuals who were significant in defining her cultural context and identity. As an example of how large familial networks are in her culture, she explained that 900 relatives attended her sister's wedding, and her mother and sisters personally wrote thank-you notes to all of them.

Another one of our assumptions is that trainees will have knowledge of the groups from which they have descended. However, many trainees of African American descent, for example, may experience difficulty tracing their roots as a result of the historical legacy of slavery. Another cultural bias has to do with our conceptualization of marriage. The cultural genogram asks trainees to identify intercultural marriages, but the term marriage is ambiguous. In Western cultures, marriage refers to a legally sanctioned union, but in other cultures the definition of marriage (and of legal) varies. The failure to make this distinction constitutes a bias.

These brief descriptions highlight the caution that should be exercised before attempting to fit "a square peg in a round hole," an attempt that characterizes most cross-cultural interactions. It is our hope that the cultural genogram, despite its cultural biases, will assist trainees and trainers alike in better knowing what it is they do not know. We believe that this process will contribute to the development of future generations of family therapists who will possess the cultural awareness and sensitivity necessary to meet the needs of an increasingly diverse clinical population.

NOTE

1   A few minor changes have been made to this reprint to establish sharper compliance with the formatting for this publication. We have changed: "article" to "chapter"; "Figure 1" to "Figure 8.1"; and removed the outdated contact information for the authors.

REFERENCES

Bahr, K. (1990). Student Responses to Genogram and Family Chronology. *Family Relations*, *39*(3), 243–249.
Carter, E. A., & Orfandis, M. (1976). Family Therapy with Only One Person and the Therapist's Own Family. In P. Guerin (Ed.), *Family therapy* (pp. 197–199). New York, NY: Gardner.
Doherty, W. J., & Baird, M. A. (1983). *Family Therapy and Family Medicine*. New York, NY: Guilford Press.
Falicov, C. J. (1988). Learning to Think Culturally. In H. Liddle, D. Breulin, & D. Schwartz (Eds.), *Handbook of Family Therapy Training and Supervision* (pp. 335–357). New York, NY: Guilford Press.
Guerin, P. J., & Pendagast, E. G. (1976). Evaluation of Family System and Genogram. In P. J. Guerin (Ed.), *Family Therapy* (pp. 450–464). New York, NY: Gardner.
Hardy, K. V. (1990). Effective Treatment of Minority Families. *Family Therapy News*, *21*(5), 5.
Hartman, A. (1977). Diagrammatic Assessment of Family Relationships. *Social Casework*, *59*, 465–476.
Jolly, W., Froom, J., & Rosen, M. G. (1980). The Genogram. *The Journal of Family Practice*, *10*(2), 251–255.
Kramer, J. R. (1985). *Family Interfaces: Transgenerational Patterns*. New York, NY: Brunner/Mazel.
Lappin, J. (1983). On Becoming a Culturally Conscious Family Therapist. In C. J. Falicov (Ed.), *Cultural Perspectives in Family Therapy* (pp. 122–136). Rockville, MD: Aspen.
Lewis, K. G. (1989) The Use of Color-Coded Genograms in Family Therapy. *Journal of Marital and Family Therapy*, *15*, 169–176.
McGoldrick, M., & Gerson. R. (1985). *Genograms in Family Assessment*. New York, NY: Norton.
Milhorn, H. T. (1981). The Genogram: A Structured Approach to the Family History. *Journal of the Mississippi State Medical Association*, *10*, 250–252.

Pendagast, E. G., & Sherman, C. O. (1977). A Guide to the Genogram. *The Family*, *5*, 101–112.

Preli, R., & Bernard, J. M. (1993). Making Multiculturalism Relevant for Majority Culture Graduate Students. *Journal of Marital and Family Therapy*, *19*, 5–16.

Rogers, J., & Durkin, M. (1984). The Semi-Structured Genogram Interview: I Protocol; II. Evaluation. *Family Systems Medicine*, *2*(1), 176–187.

Sproul, M. S., & Gallagher, R. M. (1982). The Genogram as an Aid to Crisis Intervention. *The Journal of Family Practice*, *14*(5), 959–960.

Wachtel, E. E. (1982). The Family Psyche Over Three Generations: The Genogram Revisited. *Journal of Marital and Family Therapy*, *8*, 334–343.

Collaborative Training Tools for Supervisors and Supervisees

Nancy Steiny, PhD

This chapter appeared as an article in Practical Applications in Supervision, *the publication of the California Association of Marriage and Family Therapists (CAMFT), headquartered in San Diego, California (1998, reprinted 2010).[1] This article is copyrighted and has been reprinted with the permission of CAMFT and the author. For more information regarding CAMFT, please log on to www.camft.org.*

Currently in California, new therapists (supervisees, trainees, interns) must have 3,000 hours of supervised experience to obtain a license. The Board of Behavioral Sciences is vigilant about verifying these hours; however, until recently there has been little formal concern or dialogue about the qualifications of the supervisors. Since supervisors are the gatekeepers for those who are new to the profession, providing opportunities to further supervisors' training skills is critical. Learning new and revived techniques for supervising interns can enrich even very seasoned counselors' understanding about their own therapeutic process and practices.

New models for the supervision of therapists-in-training have moved beyond the authoritarian, all-knowing supervisor who merely identifies what has been done wrong or right. Supervisors have become coaches and collaborators rather than master instructors. The seasoned therapists' experience is invaluable to the newcomer, but in his/her role, as one of a new breed of supervisors, he/she will learn along with the intern, albeit at a more advanced level. The benefactors of this collaborative learning—where both green and seasoned therapists hone their techniques together—are the clients. Collaborative learning is a win for all parties. Perhaps the most difficult aspect of the collaborative model is the bravery required on all sides. Risk taking has always been demanded of clients and therapists-in-training, but to expect the supervisor to also take such risks is quite different.

Authoritarian supervisors were safe inside their infallibility. The intern verbally presented cases and the supervisor gave advice, "Why don't you try. . ." or "Why did you do that?" In effect, they behaved as therapists-once-removed. Conventional group supervisions also often suffer from the same "once-removed" malady. Listening and giving advice requires much less creativity and curiosity than getting inside of the trainee's role to work toward collaborative solutions.

After all, much of therapy is modeling "getting unstuck." When a combination of green and seasoned experience collaborate on a therapeutic problem, both the supervisor and intern are forced to think beyond themselves, outside of their respective boxes and comfort zones.

GETTING OFF TO A GOOD START

Supervision that begins well is more likely to end well. Supervisees come to supervision at widely different points in their learning. Each one needs help from the supervisor to customize clear, attainable goals. The supervisory relationship is full of unavoidable complexities; being explicit about the expectations on both sides eliminates many avoidable pitfalls.

Supervisors need to clearly state their expectations regarding attendance at meetings; the methods they will use to supervise, e.g., one-way mirrors, and so on. Supervisors also have the responsibility for helping interns, often through an interviewing process, to state clear goals. If the goals are vague, e.g., "To be a better therapist," a supervisor might ask, "What will you be able to do with clients that is hard for you to do now?" Interns might answer that they want to "be more focused," or "have less anxiety." This clarifying process helps the supervisor understand how to best fulfill the intern's specific needs. Simultaneously, the process helps interns take responsibility for their own learning, and for setting realistic, accomplishable goals. If the intern's goals have identifiable benchmarks, both the supervisor and intern can, in their work together, experience concrete, measurable success.

Taping, live supervision, and reflecting teams all involve close collaboration between supervisors, supervisees, and clients. Clients must give written authorization for their involvement in any of the above techniques. And they should be thoroughly oriented to the technique in which they will be participating. For the technique to have maximum effect, the client must feel a sense of power over his/her decision to participate. Often, through role-play, supervisors can help interns discover effective ways to offer these opportunities to clients.

These collaborative techniques are not appropriate for all clients. A client's history is an essential prelude to determining the client's appropriateness for any of these methods. What is best for the client remains primary.

FOUR COLLABORATIVE TECHNIQUES

New therapists—as well as clients—have very different learning styles. Thus, supervisors need to explore a variety of approaches with interns to broaden their range and repertoire.

I will discuss the following techniques: role-play, videotape, live supervision, and reflecting teams. I focus on these because I have found them to maximize supervisory creativity and collaboration. Each comes with its own unique advantages and disadvantages. Of course, supervisors should acquaint themselves with as many models of therapy skills and techniques as possible.

THE FOUR COLLABORATIVE TECHNIQUES

#1—Role-Playing

Role-playing is by no means new, but the dimension it adds to therapist-in-training skills is often overlooked.

An intern trying to describe a current client is often placed in a difficult position. While trying to present the case with clarity and honesty, the intern struggles with being objective. Life experiences and assumptions can't help but sneak in and taint the purity of the case presentation. By using role-play, the new therapist takes on the client's issues as his or her own, while "acting" in the role of the client. This "experience" is much more powerful and illuminating than a third-party report.

In the context of supervision, role-playing permits the intern to behave as they experience the client in the therapy session. One method to begin the role-play is to have the supervisor interview the trainee acting in the role of the client. Warm-up questions, such as those that follow, will help the intern get into the client's "skin."

- What's it like to be with this client?
- Does this client remind you of anyone you know?
- If you believe that this client provokes you into having an agenda for them, how would you proceed?
- How does your agenda sometimes block your curiosity in discovering the client's goals?

"Becoming" the client gives the intern experiential learning which is not bound by rational explanation. Through this experience, the new therapist gets a sense of what it's like to be in this particular client's life (Gliekauf-Hughes & Campbell, 1991).

Furthermore, role-playing gives the supervisor insight into both the trainee's ability to have a sense of the client's experience and into the trainee's ability to understand the interrelational process that exists between therapist and the client (Bugental, 1981). During the interview, with the intern as client, the supervisor models a therapeutic interviewing process which is designed to help the trainee work with this particular client.

When the supervisor has asked enough questions to get a sense of the client/therapist relationship, the supervisor may debrief the trainee by stepping out of the interviewer's role and by asking the trainee questions directly such as:

- What was it like to be this client?
- How would you describe this client's world?

If supervision is done in a group setting, the other trainees have a chance to observe the supervisor as a model. The observing trainees might also note that the intern's case is similar to a case with which they're struggling, so all participants benefit from the role-playing experience.

As an example, Mary, an intern in supervision, who was recently divorced and raw from the experience, held strong convictions about women's rights and rules that "should" govern marriage. She insisted that most women deny their real self in order to be in a marital relationship. Mary had trouble believing that her client, Irma, from El Salvador, was content and unquestioning about her relationship with her husband. Their relationship operated within a structure traditional to their culture. Irma's presenting problem was that her daughter had become too Americanized. Irma was afraid her daughter would take on values not compatible with the South American culture. By role-playing Irma, Mary could see that her therapeutic work had drifted towards her own needs and values and away from the objectives of her clients. Role-playing gave her a perspective that helped her become curious about how her personal values might hinder her from being tolerant and objective.

Role-play is equally effective in individual and group supervision. When the supervisor takes on the role of the therapist in training, that new trainee learns by experiencing what kinds of questions are most helpful. Again, through experience, a trainee can sense what questions not only establish empathy and understanding, but also empower and expand the clients' visions of themselves. Then, when the supervisor has become familiar with the client through role-play, he or she may reverse roles and play the client, putting the trainee back into the role of therapist.

In group supervision, when the members become more comfortable with each other, other trainees may offer to play the therapist while the case presenter plays his or her client. Obviously, the "therapist" and "client" are never played to perfection. However, the role-play exercise reveals much about the supervisee's stage of development, natural talents, competency, and observational skills. As the client, the trainee is "trying it on" so he can see how certain actions might evoke certain types of thoughts, or how a client might think and feel in order to create certain actions. "Trying it on" helps diffuse the intern's defensiveness and anxiety. The learning comes from literally being the client, for a moment, and not from a disembodied case description. When playing the role of therapist, the supervisor implicitly gives feedback to the intern in an atmosphere promoting cooperation rather than one that invites tiresome battles (overt or covert) with trainees. Role-playing helps supervisees to connect empathetically with their clients, and to learn the client's response to the therapist's style of questioning. Similarly, role-playing helps supervisors connect more empathically with their trainees.

#2—Videotaping

Nearly since they came on the commercial market, videotapes have been popular among therapists. Videotaping enhances therapists' effectiveness with clients. Therapists have considered the ability to tape and view their own clinical work as a contribution to their own professional development. But equally important and often overlooked, is the evolving use of videotaping in supervision—a feedback process which truly enriches the training (Breunlin, Karrer, McGuire & Cimmarusti, 1988). With videotaping, interns are no longer limited to their recollections of prior therapy sessions. While viewing a tape, the supervisor and intern have access to the non-verbal behaviors of therapist and client. Re-playing permits sessions to be studied in detail. Re-playing a tape is a form of self-confrontation (Heilveil & Muehleman, 1981). When more than one person views a tape, there can be multiple viewpoints. Often when the supervisor and trainee exchange views about the video, new approaches to the therapeutic process evolve, giving the therapist-in-training more options for interacting with the client.

Videotaping is useful with any theoretical framework. Viewing a therapist's work has the capacity to teach trainees both theory and technique and helps trainees to trust, monitor, and develop their own styles and abilities.

Yes, obtaining video equipment involves an initial expense. But when used correctly, videotapes offer one of the richest learning experiences an intern (and a supervisor) can have. "If used correctly" is key, because complexities do arise when using video.

First and foremost, trainees respond more positively when the supervisors are willing to be taped, preferably showing an early, unedited and imperfect segment. Interns tend to think of supervisors as "knowing it all," so exposure to the supervisor's fallibility and vulnerability will ease the intern's tension and anxiety. Second, before viewing a trainee's tape, ask the trainee to outline how he/she would like to receive feedback. The trainee's sense of empowerment over his/her feedback will contribute toward easing anxiety. For example, a counselor was asked to describe desired feedback. He replied that all he wanted was to be told how wonderful he was because he'd had a bad day. After viewing his tape, he was given the "wonderful feedback." He then went on to say, "I'm feeling better now and would like some helpful guidelines." Interns who are in charge of their feedback are much more likely to be curious and less defensive.

Third, an intern should preview the tape on his/her own. When an intern has seen his/her tape, he/she might pick, for example, two five-minute segments to show to the supervision group—one he/she really liked, and one where he/she is seeking assistance from the group. The explanations for picking each choice can be revealing. The trainee might begin to explore other therapeutic avenues or to ask questions about how the more difficult selection might have been improved. This previewing process helps the new therapist clarify and mentally organize what he or she might want from the supervision. Unless trainees take some responsibility for what is helpful for their learning and development, the supervisor's efforts can easily backfire, producing defensiveness, anxiety and little learning.

Fourth, after the intern has designed a format for feedback, viewed the tape, and selected the two segments, the supervisor might prepare for the more complete viewing by asking the intern a few clarifying questions. Some examples might be:

- What were some of your observations that you liked while you were viewing the tape?
- What will help you lessen your critical voice when we view this tape together?
- What is your inner experience of being with this particular client?
- How do you think your internal reactions to this client influenced the questions you asked?
- What was going on in you [therapist] that helped you design this particular question?
- What was the process you used to organize the client's information that gave you a meaningful way to proceed?
- How did you use the client's feedback process to continue in this session?

For videotaping to be effective as a learning tool, a supervisor must pay careful attention to establishing a positive atmosphere of learning. The time interns spend on designing their goals and preferred manner of feedback is an excellent investment.

#3—Live Supervision (Using a One-Way Mirror)

For supervisors (and fellow interns) to observe a live, in-progress therapy session is immediate, effective and potent. At first, therapists such as Minuchin and Haley (among others) who were experimenting with a new concept of family therapy, used one-way mirrors to demonstrate their work to one another (Heilveil & Muehleman, 1981). From this beginning, live supervision eventually evolved as a training tool.

One-way mirrors have been around since the early 1950s, but these eminently useful tools are under used. Of course, the initial expense of installing such a device stops many struggling agencies. A one-way mirror requires two rooms: one for observation, and one for the actual interaction with the client. Many anxious supervisors avoid the opportunity out of fear that it will become unmanageable and personally exposing.

In the days of authoritarian supervision, the supervisor would often use the phone connection between the observation and the interviewing room to interrupt and give directions to the intern. These interruptions understandably produced anxiety. Sometimes supervisors would direct the therapist to leave the interviewing room for a consultation with the supervisor. Perhaps most invasive (Gershenson & Cohen, 1978), the supervisor would enter the interviewing room after a designated period of time to participate in the session. At that time theory held that these practices helped avoid major therapeutic mistakes, especially preventing the therapist from becoming "enmeshed" in the client's system. Therefore today, using one-way mirrors as a supervisory tool requires a careful approach.

Supervisors must create an atmosphere where fear of evaluations quickly dissolves into an environment of collaborating with colleagues for the benefit of clients. Fortunately, the work of Anderson and Goolishian (1988), White and Epstein (1988), and Tom Anderson

(1987) have moved beyond rigid and intrusive practices to develop highly effective, collaborative methods of training new therapists with live viewing making the process of therapy more public and the therapist more accountable to the profession (Young, 1989, 1990).

Because mirror work is rarely used in private practice, the following discussion is primarily for the benefit of agency settings. As a mode of supervision, live observation is more intense and condensed than case reporting and discussion. Information is immediate and thus must be processed and used quickly (Berger & Dummunn, 1982). Live supervision is complex and has possibilities for both technical and interpersonal difficulties. Thus, several conditions must be met to create a safe learning atmosphere for interns. As with videotaping, the supervisor must be the first to be observed by the supervision group. A good start would be for the interns to observe their supervisor doing an initial agency intake. A veteran supervisor's seasoned demonstration conveys much technical information and role modeling. To augment this learning opportunity, interns can write questions about areas of confusion or disagreement that might have come up while observing their supervisor. Thus, the supervisor is the first to be put into a position of modeling non-defensive responses to the suggestions and questions of others.

Again, so that supervisors can intervene in a way that will benefit the clients' therapy and promote the supervisees' growth, it is extremely important that the intern therapist behind the mirror design his/her desired feedback. By empowering the therapist under observation, the supervision ambiance will change from one of "gotcha" judgment and criticism to one of "we are a team working together for the benefit of clients." Interns' apprehensions about power and control issues with supervisors dissipate considerably once supervisees feel respected and empowered by their supervisors. A supervisor can offer an intern a list of options in pre-session discussions. For example:

- What would be most helpful for you during the session?
- Would you want some phone calls, none, or only when you feel stuck?
- Would you like a reflecting team today?
- Are there any of your goals you would like us to pay special attention to today?
- What style of feedback during our time together has been most useful to you?

Each question can be designed to enhance the intern's awareness of his/her own process and needs.

In an atmosphere of empowerment and collaboration, live supervision can significantly accelerate a trainee's growth as a therapist. Different styles and skills become immediately obvious by observing colleagues and supervisor. A trainee's experience both in front of and behind the screen offers two very different, but valid views of the same coin. Interns explore different ways of receiving and asking for support. The experience offers such intensified learning for interns that their initial stage fright quickly changes to curiosity and a yearning to grow and be independent, See Storm and Todd (1997) for a detailed discussion of the ways to promote a supervisee's development and autonomy and the ways that do not.

When using one-way mirrors for the first time, supervisors usually experience a process similar to the interns—evolving from performance anxiety to a gradual feeling of being part of a team. Supervisors, like interns, quickly improve their ability to fulfill their responsibilities as trainers. As the supervisor notices and comments on the trainees' strengths, trainees increasingly focus on empowering their clients.

Anyone unfamiliar with using a one-way mirror may worry about its effect on clients. In a research study (Piercy, Sprenkle & Constantine, 1986), clients reported a positive reaction to live supervision, indicating that they felt two or more heads were better than one. Of course, not all clients are appropriate for participating in this technique. And, the client must voluntarily choose to participate. Usually when therapists become comfortable with the mirror, so do their clients.

#4—Reflecting Teams

We have Tom Anderson (1990) to thank for his concept and explanations of the use of reflecting teams. Anderson makes clear that reflecting teams are not so much a "method" as they are a way of thinking—a way of putting ideas into action.

A reflecting team is usually made up of at least one supervisor and fellow interns, working together to provide feedback from various points of view. Teams might work with or without a one-way mirror. Clients are offered the opportunity to work with a team as an adjunct to their work with the therapist. A clear explanation of the team concept gives the client power over the decision as to whether he/she believes the process will be useful.

Reflecting teams are inappropriate for some clients. For others, the introduction of reflecting teams needs to be timed sensitively. Some clients having experienced reflecting teams immediately request further sessions in this format. Many express their enthusiasm about having several therapists involved in their therapeutic progress. Clients should be offered the option to meet the team before the therapist begins the session. Permission to use a reflecting team should be obtained from clients in writing.

A typical reflecting team session begins with the therapist and client(s) interacting in therapeutic conversation for perhaps a half an hour or until a break seems appropriate. At that time, either the therapist will ask the client(s) if it seems like the right time to hear from the team, or the team will announce its readiness to respond. If the therapist, the client(s) or the team chooses to decline an invitation for a reflection, it is, of course, respected.

Some agencies have facilities capable of switching light and bringing sound into the consulting room. This mechanical method is expensive to install. Equally useful and more accessible is merely having the team switch rooms whereby the client(s) and the therapist move to the observational side. Before switching, the therapist might say to the client(s), "The team has some comments on what they have observed. Some of their thoughts may be useful and others may not." When the client(s) and therapist have heard the team's reflections, the participants switch back to their original rooms. At that point, the team now hears the client(s)' comments. The therapist may start the conversation by asking the client, "What, if any, of the teams comments stood out for you or seemed helpful?"

The objective of team reflection is to give the client(s) and therapist an opportunity to sit back and hear alternative meanings or issues raised during the clinical interview (Tomm, 1991). Often the experience allows client(s) and therapist to see themselves, their actions, and their relationships in new ways. Reflecting often helps both client(s) and trainee loosen their tenacity to the one view they have found credible which broadens the behavioral and therapeutic options. Teams are coached to offer reflections that are liberating, not corrective or prescriptive.

The method of working with reflecting teams tends to be very respectful of clients since they not only get to observe the team's reflections, but also have the opportunity to comment on the team's observations. This allows the clients to pick and choose as to which of the teams' tentative wondering and ideas are most likely to be therapeutic and useful. Each team member codes and collects information differently, so clients have the option to view their relationships and problems from various perspectives.

These new meanings and perspectives are also available to the therapist, supervisor and members of the team (interns). Team members are discouraged from talking to each other during the observation to avoid developing a sense that any one team member's construction is "right." As team members, trainees learn that their views are neither right nor wrong and that these differences promote creativity and self-confidence. By removing most of the hierarchical structure of supervision, collaborating on speculative reflections stirs the interns' curiosity on many levels and expedites their growth as therapists. Both therapists and supervisors have expressed relief at working in a team format. No one person carries the load of working with difficult clients. Supervisees respond very positively to this collaborative model and find it useful in their own clinical growth. This more open way of working quickly exposes secret agendas that interns might unknowingly be imposing on clients. Reflecting teams push trainees to learn and have curiosity about the use of language when forming questions that influence the interaction between themselves and their clients.

BECOMING A SUPERVISOR GUARANTEES A QUANTUM LEAP IN PROFESSIONAL DEVELOPMENT

Clearly, the transition from being a therapist to being a supervisor requires a significant leap in thinking, skills, and professional identity (Borders, 1992). Merely taking charge over an intern's training is hugely different from taking responsibility for it. Being a good supervisor requires more than good will. The field badly needs risk-takers willing to give up a comfortable authority to work shoulder to shoulder with interns. Only by challenging themselves and their own positions will supervisors create a professional culture dedicated to continuous growth among seasoned and novice therapists. The primary benefactor of this culture will be the client.

NOTE

1   A few minor changes have been made to this reprint to establish sharper compliance with the formatting of this publication.

REFERENCES

Anderson, H., & Goolishian, H. (1988). Human Systems as Linguistic Systems: Preliminary and Evolving Ideas About the Implications for Clinical Theory. *Family Process, 27*(4), 371–394.

Anderson, T. (1987). The Reflecting Team: Dialogue and Meta-Dialogue in Clinical Work, *Family Process, 26*, 415–428.

Anderson, T. (1990). *The Reflecting Team Dialogues*. Kent, UK: Borgmann Publishing.

Berger, M., & Dummunn, C. (1982). Live Supervision as Context, Treatment and Training. *Family Process, 21*, 337–344.

Borders, D. L. (1992). Learning to Think Like a Supervisor. *The Clinical Supervisor, 10*(2), 135–148.

Breunlin D., Karrer, B., McGuire, D., & Cimmarusti, R. (1988). Cybernetics of Videotape Supervision. In H. Liddle, D. Breunlin, & R. Schwartz (Eds.), *Handbook of Family Therapy Training and Supervision* (pp. 194–206). New York, NY: Guilford Press.

Bugental, J. F. T. (1981). *The Search for Authenticity: An Existential-Analytic Approach to Psychotherapy* (rev. ed.). New York, NY: Irvington.

Gershenson, J., & Cohen, M. S. (1978). Through the Looking Glass: The Experience of Two Family Therapy Trainees with Live Supervision. *Family Process, 17*(2), 225–230.

Gliekauf-Hughes, C., & Campbell, L. R. (1991). Experiential Supervision; Applied Techniques for a Case Presentation Approach. *Psychotherapy, 28*(4).

Heilveil, I., & Muehleman, J. (1981). Nonverbal Clues to Deception in Psychotherapy Analogue. *Psychotherapy, Theory, Research and Practice, 18*(3), 329–335.

Piercy, F., Sprenkle, D., & Constantine, J. (1986). Family Members' Perceptions of Live Observation/ Supervision. *Contemporary Family Therapy—An International Journal, 8*, 171–187.

Protinsky, H. (1997). Dismounting the Tiger: Using Tape in Supervision. *The Complete Systemic Supervision* (pp. 298–307). Boston, MA: Allyn & Bacon.

Storm, C. L. & Todd, T. C. (1997). Live Supervision Revolutionizes the Supervision Process. *The Complete Systemic Supervision*, (pp. 283–297) Boston, MA: Allyn & Bacon.

Todd, T. C., & Storm, C. L. (2014). *The Complete Systemic Supervisor: Context, Philosophy, and Pragmatics* (2nd ed.). Malden, MA: Wiley.

Tomm, K. (1991). *Orienting Notes for Members of a Reflecting Team*. An unpublished manuscript.

White, M., & Epston, D. (1989). *Literate Means to Therapeutic Ends*. Adelaide, South Australia: Dulwich Centre Publications.

Young, J. (1989/1990). A Critical Look at the One-Way Screen. *Dulwich Centre Newsletter*, Summer, 5–11.

10

Promoting Cultural Sensitivity in Online and Electronically-Based Supervision

Kenneth V. Hardy, PhD

Online supervision seems to be a major nascent trend in our field and beyond. Because of the extensive "reach" of technology, online supervision holds tremendous potential for bringing together a widely heterogeneous group of supervisees who can theoretically interact with each other from different corners of the world or make supervision available to those in remote geographical areas where supervisory resources may be limited. With the proper care, planning, and creativity, online supervision can be an important mechanism for providing culturally sensitive supervision.

This chapter identifies a number of broad parameters that are important to consider when designing and implementing an online approach to supervision geared towards promoting cultural sensitivity. It is important to note that the major thrust of the chapter is to provide a snapshot of how to integrate and promote cultural sensitivity within an online approach to supervision. The suggestions contained within this chapter are predicated on the notion that supervisors are well versed in both supervision and online instruction and technology.

The following is a list of guidelines for incorporating cultural sensitivity into online and other distance learning approaches to supervision:

1. Establish an explicit contract highlighting the commitment to culturally sensitive supervision. This is a crucial first step and it is imperative that the supervisor operationally defines what this means and how it will shape the supervisory process and relationship. Supervisees should be informed that supervision will not be relegated to case reports but will also involve intense self of the therapist work that will draw heavily from a host of didactic-experiential exercises that will be an integral part of the process.

2. Clearly define the parameters and core values associated with an approach to supervision centered on cultural sensitivity. These values include: a) understanding one's self as a cultural being; b) a focus on the self of the therapist/supervisor issues; c) an examination of self in relationship to other; d) talking openly, honestly, and uninhibitedly about the varied dimensions of culture; e) exploring and hypothesizing how presenting problems and the process of therapy may be informed, compounded,

exacerbated, and/or ameliorated by one or more dimension(s) of culture; f) willingness to utilize self-disclosure and establishing comfort with it from all participants involved in the supervisory process, including the supervisor; g) participation in regular experiential exercises that may appear tangential but that are key to enhancing cultural awareness and sensitivity; h) access to raw clinical data via video streaming, audiotapes, or other technologies; i) agreement to a 9–12 month contract for supervision; and j) understanding and attending to the dynamics of power, powerlessness, privilege, and subjugation.

3. Require all supervisees to complete, post, and be prepared to discuss their genograms very early in the supervisory process, preferably by no later than the second or third session. When conducted early in the process, it sets the appropriate tone by reinforcing this as a core value by privileging self-exploration as a precursor to clinical effectiveness.

4. Take appropriate measures to ensure confidentiality of the process and be explicit about the possible limitations of it, when applicable. It is important for the supervisor to specifically and concretely address how confidentiality will be ensured and maintained throughout the process.

5. Conduct ongoing evaluation and regular supervisory feedback sessions. As is the case with all supervision regardless of format or modality, establishing a strong and viable feedback loop between the supervisor and supervisee is critical. This is especially crucial with those approaches to online supervision where there may be limited or no access to raw data or visuals.

When online supervision involves the simultaneous participation of multiple supervisees, the process of promoting cultural sensitivity would adhere to the same process that would be in place for face-to-face group supervision. The simultaneous participation of multiple supervisees would ensure that there are ample opportunities to foster experiential learning, which is critical to promoting cultural sensitivity. Building experiential learning into the supervisory process is one of the major challenges of online supervision especially if/when it is provided to an individual.

PROMOTING CULTURALLY SENSITIVE ONLINE SUPERVISION WITH INDIVIDUAL SUPERVISEES: TWO INTERRELATED PHASES

The supervision process is organized into two interrelated phases: The Pre-Supervision Phase and the Supervisory Engagement Phase. The Pre-Supervision Phase is a "business type" meeting where all of the logistics and expectations regarding the supervision are carefully outlined. It is during this phase that the supervisee is introduced to the rudiments of the Multicultural Relational Perspective along with a brief overview of the core values and the training philosophy. Since this supervisory approach is a little different from traditional approaches to supervision, and is heavily geared towards self of the therapist work, it is essential that all prospective supervisees know exactly what the process will involve. The Supervisory Engagement Phase is structured to provide the necessary clinical oversight for supervision. These two phases are detailed as follows.

Pre-Supervision Phase

The prospective supervisee is provided with a "Promoting Cultural Sensitivity Starter Kit" which is to be read during the Pre-Supervision Phase of the process. The Kit provides the prospective supervisee with a thorough overview of the conceptual tools needed for the online supervision sessions. The PCS Starter Kit contains the following:

- MRP Core Beliefs and Values Handout.
- Explanation of Multidimensional Self Handout.
- Location of Self Handout.
- Homework Policy Handout.
- Cultural Genogram Handout.
- Resources for More Information about Genograms.

Once the handouts are read, the supervisee should be prepared to discuss the contents of the Starter Kit with the supervisor and sign a Letter of Understanding and Consent, which may constitute the *Supervisory Contract*, unless otherwise indicated by the supervisor and/or supervisee.

Please note that the PCS Starter Kit may be found in the *Handouts and Resources* section of this Manual.

Engagement Phase

Once the *Supervisory Contract* has been executed, the process advances to the Engagement Phase. It is important for the online sessions to be structured to provide the necessary clinical oversight that is expected in supervision as well as include time and space for exercises that will promote cultural sensitivity. Since it is often difficult to simultaneously provide adequate clinical oversight and implement exercises designed to promote cultural sensitivity, it is strongly recommended that online and electronically-based supervisory experiences are negotiated for a minimum of 90 minutes to ensure sufficient time.

The following section provides a 10-session *Sample Curriculum* of how issues of diversity can be integrated into the online supervisory process with an individual supervisee. The list is provided for illustration purposes only and thus is a guideline and is not intended to be prescriptive.

SAMPLE CURRICULUM

Session One

- The session starts with introductions and a general check-in. Once this is completed, the supervisee may be asked to answer the following questions *before* presenting a case:

1. How many siblings, if any, did you have in the family you grew up in?
2. Where were you in the sibling order?
3. How did growing up with [n] siblings shape or contribute to your values, temperament, attitudes, personality and/or philosophy of life?
4. How did growing up as [nth] (sibling position) shape your outlook, perspective, or view of the world?
5. What contributions have your sibling position and experiences made to your gifts and struggles as a therapist?

- Once these family-of-origin (FOO) questions are explored, the supervisee may then be invited to present a case for discussion. The supervisor will discuss the dynamics of the case in adherence with his or her theoretical orientation and as the clinical circumstances warrant. However, it is important that, at some point during the case discussion, the supervisor makes an earnest attempt to integrate the self of the therapist discussion into the clinical conversation about the case. For example, the supervisor might simply ask: "What impact, if any, do you think the dynamics associated with the sibling subsystem might have on the a) formation of the presenting problem; b) the maintenance of the problem; and/or c) the therapeutic process?" As is often the case, the questions that are asked in supervision are often so much more significant than the answers that are produced. In this regard, the significance of the supervisor's questions is to nurture the development of the following conceptual skills that are crucial to promoting cultural sensitivity: a) Self in relation to other reflection; b) thinking relationally; c) thinking contextually; and d) the location of self and use of self.

Homework Assignment: Assign genogram construction homework that is to be presented during the third session.

Session Two

- It is customary to start the supervision session with a general "check-in" with a discussion of any reflections or residuals from the previous session. A relevant check-in question might be: "Did you have any additional reflections, insights, memories, etc. about your sibling relationships or position? What about any other thoughts about your client(s)?"

- The supervisor initiates a conversation about gender and invites deeper reflection. How did gender play out in the family you grew up in? What were the gender-related observations, implicit and explicit messages you experienced that influenced who you are today and how you think of yourself as a gendered being, if you do in fact think of yourself in this way? How did gender shape the relationships between you and your sibling(s)?

- The supervisor may also initiate a conversation about *preferred gender pronouns* to be used in supervision and in the supervisory relationship with each other. Consistent with the MRP, the supervisor assumes the *broker of permission* role and initiates the conversation by disclosing: "My preferred gender pronoun in relationship to my identity is 'he or him.' Do you have a preferred pronoun?"

- Once again, following the self of the therapist conversation, the supervisor is now poised to seamlessly transition to the case presentation. Whether it is the same case from the previous session, a new case, or a combination of cases, it is the supervisor's role to ensure that the two contextual variables that have been introduced into supervision, FOO and gender, are considered within the conceptualization of the dynamics of the case and the treatment plan(s). Similarly, another crucial task of the supervisor is to encourage the supervisee to critically examine relevant self of the therapist issues that could possibly facilitate and/or hinder the therapeutic process.

- At no point during the supervision should the implementation of the strategies for promoting cultural awareness and sensitivity deter a supervisor from establishing fidelity with his or her theoretical orientation. The self of the therapist exercises are designed to challenge and encourage the supervisee to consider how the nuances of culture are intricately intertwined into virtually all aspects of therapy.

Homework Assignment: *Please identify two examples of how you believe your perception is shaped by your gender and two examples of how you believe how you are perceived is influenced by your gender.*

Session Three

- Once again it is standard practice to commence the new supervision session with a check-in question, reflection, etc.

- The majority of this session is devoted to the supervisee presenting her or his genogram to the supervisor, who is listening for themes and looking for patterns as a means of helping the supervisee become adept at doing the same. The genogram presentation is also designed to assist the supervisee with the following: a) sharpen one's view for recognizing patterns; b) develop a more acute and complex understanding of one's self and family history; c) "build one's muscles" for tolerating and enduring both intimacy (i.e., vulnerability) and intensity (discomfort); e) increase one's aptitude and capacity for embracing relational and contextual thinking; and f) promote critical thinking and greater understanding regarding how both challenging and rewarding family experiences can be powerful therapeutic resources when they have been appropriately addressed.

- The genogram presentation is assigned early on in the supervisory relationship and delayed until the third session deliberately. The two previous sessions are really structured to prepare the supervisee for the cultural genogram presentation. The queries about sibling positioning and gender are designed to encourage the supervisee to begin thinking critically about family patterns and more importantly to develop a facility and comfort with the rudimentary stages of self-exploration. The genogram presentation nudges the process of self-exploration to a slightly more advanced state. It is important for the supervisor to remind the supervisee that the cultural genogram is a "living document" that will necessitate modifications, updates, and so forth. As such, there will be additional times throughout the course of supervision where the supervisee will be called upon to present aspects of the genogram again.

- The remaining portion of the session should be devoted to case presentation/ consultation. Once again, it is the role of the supervisor to ensure that the session is coherent for the supervisee. The connections between the supervisee's genogram presentation and his or her clinical work should be seamless and well integrated. Although a sharp and narrow focus on the clinical work has been compromised by the attention that has been devoted to self of the therapist issues, the supervisee's work by now should begin to demonstrate a greater appreciation for the complexity of human suffering and how it is interwoven with contextual factors.

- As the supervision sessions continue, the supervisee, if applying "lessons learned" and "tidbits" from each session, should be demonstrating an enhanced ability to present and examine clinical case dynamics with increasing attention to and appreciation for the interconnectedness of contextual factors, the presenting problem, and therapeutic process.

> **Homework Assignment**: Please "interview" at least one family member to address a remaining question you have about your genogram or family history.

Session Four

- Following the routine check-in, the supervisor initiates a conversation about religion. The supervisee is invited and encouraged to think about and share how his or her attitudes, beliefs, and ultimately therapy/supervision might be (negatively and/or positively) shaped by religion. Even if the supervisee does not participate in or belong to a specific religion, this conversation is an important one to have. Religion is a major organizing principle in United States culture that underpins virtually all aspects of our society while remaining nearly impossible to openly discuss. This topic is usually intentionally deferred until later in the supervisory process because it may require a little more prodding by the supervisor, which can be facilitated by a solid supervisor-supervisee relationship. Moreover, it is also critical and customary during this process for the supervisor to refer the supervisee back to his or her respective genogram as a means of generating additional thoughts, questions, and reflections, and as a potential pathway to deepening the conversation.

- Once the supervisor has effectively exercised the *Broker of Permission* role by initiating and participating in a progressive conversation about religion, it paves the way for a host of other relevant issues to be critically explored. Some of these might include: a) What do you think might be the advantages and disadvantages of treating a client whose religion is different from/the same as yours?; b) What do you think it would be like for you if/when you have a client whose religiously based beliefs clash with a personal view you might have?; and c) what would be a clinical scenario in which a client might have a personal view or behavior that clashes with your religious views?

- Once again, it is imperative that the conversation about religion and the self-exploration that accompanies it not only builds on previous contextual and clinical conversations but it must also be done in a way that weaves it all into an integrated whole. The supervisor must assume an important and major responsibility in ensuring that this happens.

- This session culminates with a clinical case presentation and discussion. While the clinical dynamics of the case will always dictate the course of action, if any, recommended by the supervisor, a keen consideration of the relevant contextual variables must also be an integral part of the overall supervisory process.

Homework Assignment: Based on our discussion today, what significance, if any, do you believe there is in factoring religion into the therapeutic and supervisory equations?

Session Five

- It is rare in our society to engage in a conversation about religion without issues germane to sexual orientation being implicated and vice versa. Thus, following the routine check-in portion of the session, the supervisor shifts the focus to the topic of sexual orientation. Unlike with the other topics thus far, the supervisee is *not* asked to disclose his or her sexual identity or orientation. Despite some societal progress made towards the acceptance of the LGBTQ community, it is still not a completely safe world for anyone who is not or who is presumed not to be heterosexual. Thus a major focal point of the exploration during this session is on the centrality of heterosexuality and heterosexism and how they consciously and unconsciously inform our language, perceptions, and behaviors inside and outside of therapy/ supervision. These conversations, the unpacking of what it means to be heterosexual and the examination of heterosexism, are crucial conversations to have especially for those who identify as heterosexual. During these important and intense conversations, it is often common for many gay, lesbian, bi-sexual, and transgendered supervisees to voluntarily self-disclose, although this is neither the intent nor necessarily the desired outcome of the exploration. However, when this level of sharing does occur, it may also serve as an important indicator that substantial progress has been made in the establishment of trust in the supervisory relationship.

- It cannot be emphasized enough how important it is for the supervisor to stitch all of these seemingly fragmented conversations, reflections, and explorations together in a coherent way. This process is central to promoting cultural sensitivity when supervising online in isolation, without the benefit of the consistent interactional and experiential dynamics often fostered by the presence of other supervisees.

- During the case presentation portion of this session, it is important for the supervisor to encourage the supervisee to consider how the intersections of gender, sexual orientation, sexual identity, religion, and FOO dynamics are threaded throughout the case. This is not to suggest that any one or any of these would constitute the reason a given client is seeking treatment or that any of these is "a problem" in the therapy or supervision. Instead, the supervisee continues to build on a developing awareness and sensitivity that contextual factors provide a lens through which we all see the world, consciously and/or unconsciously, and through which we are seen.

> **Homework Assignment**: Before our next session, please review your genogram and consider what are the implicit and explicit rules regarding heterosexuality that shape your family's and your culture's attitudes, beliefs, and behaviors. How might these "rules" welcome or alienate a LGBTQ family member?

Session Six

- While it is important for the supervisor to constantly facilitate the integration of all of the dimensions of culture throughout the supervisory process, the sixth session is usually designated to highlighting intersectionality. This process typically starts following the standard check-in process.

- During this session, the supervisor may commence the case presentation discussion a little earlier than what is customary. The supervisee is asked to discuss in a much more systemic and holistic fashion the ways in which the case dynamics shape and are shaped by the various dimensions of culture. While each of the previous sessions is designed to build on one another and the supervisory conversations are expected to reflect both the progression and integration, this session constitutes a type of "midterm" examination for the supervisee and the supervisor. It is a built-in mechanism to determine the extent to which the supervisee is developing and/or refining the executive skills of *thinking culturally* and *thinking relationally*. This session is a critical step in further assisting the supervisor to gauge the pace of the supervision and the progress of the supervisee, particularly in terms of developing a heightened sense of cultural awareness and sensitivity. While the *evaluation process* is ongoing and occurs naturally throughout the supervisory process, having a clearly demarcated designated check-in session such as this one, affords the supervisee and supervisor an opportunity to be explicit and intentional with each other in discussing the progress of the process to date. Since online and electronic approaches to supervision often lack the benefit of granting a supervisor the same access to the numerous subtleties of human communication that is often so invaluable in face-to-face encounters, a designated session like this becomes even more crucial, especially to relationship building.

- By the conclusion of this session, the supervisor generally has a more crystalized view of how the process should proceed. In some cases, the supervision may need "rebooting" because it may have been stalled or stuck along the way. In other instances, it may be determined that it is progressing at an appropriate pace and in concert with the developmental needs of the supervisee. It is also conceivable that there are powerful indicators to suggest that the pace can or needs to be accelerated.

***Homework Assignment**: Based on our session today, please identify one new learning or insight you had about yourself as a therapist, a supervisee, me as your supervisor, and about your work with your client.*

Session Seven

- To further facilitate the focus on intersectionality, this session is devoted to the exploration of the cultural genogram. Following the customary pre-session check-in, the supervisee is encouraged to provide an overview of his or her cultural genogram. This presentation builds on the earlier discussions pursuant to the Family of Origin Genogram but takes a much sharper, concentrated and deliberate examination of the influences of culture. While the cultural genogram embraces all dimensions of culture, ethnicity is highlighted. For some supervisees, especially African Americans whose ethnic identities have been obscured and obliterated by the legacy of slavery, this conversation may be conflated with issues of race.

- In concert with the standard processing of the cultural genogram, the supervisee is encouraged to identify his or her cultural (ethnic) background and to discuss and explore the following: a) the major organizing principles associated with his or her cultural background (which could conceivably be comprised of several different ethnicities); b) pride issues associated with one's cultural background; and c) culturally-based shame issues. It is imperative during this process that the supervisor assists the supervisee in remaining sharply focused on *culture of origin* in a way that does not become clouded by *family of origin* issues. Although there is considerable overlap between the two, there are also some distinctive features that would be important to help the supervisee differentiate. For example, it is possible that a supervisee could have grown up in a family with a history of family secrets that might be rooted in a history of incest and sexual abuse that may have nothing to do with one's cultural heritage. Given such a scenario, it would be important for the supervisor to encourage the supervisee to explore *if* and *how* the family pattern of incest was connected to the cultural heritage of the family. It would obfuscate the role of the cultural genogram, if for example, the supervisee declared the incest to be a shame issue associated with his or her culture rather than a behavior uniquely connected to one's family of origin rather than one's culture (which is generally more universal).

- During the case presentation segment of the supervision, it is important for the supervisor to encourage the supervisee to consider how the dynamics of culture are contributing to the overall therapeutic process. It would also be important for the supervisor to encourage the supervisee to be curious about what dimensions of the client's behavior might be understood differently, and perhaps even better, once considered within the context of culture. The same invitation would be extended to the supervisee to consider with regards to his or her culture as well.

Homework Assignment: *Please identify three cultural traits that are integral to your cultural background and three traits that are integral to the cultural background of one of your clients.*

Session Eight

- The session begins with a check-in, followed by a review and discussion of the homework assignment. The discussion of culture, particularly against the backdrop of all of the other dimensions of diversity that have been explored up until this point, paves the way for an in-depth conversation about race. In many ways, of all the dimensions of culture that are integrated throughout the supervisory process, race is always among the most challenging and difficult to unpack. Our society's complex and protracted history of denying the saliency of race while simultaneously being profoundly organized by it adds to the difficulty of talking about it both in and outside of supervision.

- The supervisor can play an instrumental role in launching a conversation about race by identifying one's racial identity and also disclosing how it informs him or her as a supervisor as well as one's approach to supervision. It is important for the supervisor to be thoughtful and explicit in discussing where one's racial identity places him or her on the racial privilege-subjugation spectrum. Whether one is racially privileged or subjugated, it is crucial for the supervisor to acknowledge and share his or her positioning while also pointing out how it *might* shape one's attitudes, beliefs, and behaviors in supervision and beyond.

- Once the supervisor has laid the groundwork for a discussion about race via supervisory self-disclosure, the supervisee is then invited to participate in a conversation about race. The supervisor can facilitate the process by asking the supervisee: "How do you identify racially?" Most supervisees, especially those who are White, will need considerable guidance and assistance with this process. It is also important for the supervisor to be vigilant in staying the course and making sure that it is indeed race that is explored and not another related issue. Thus typical answers such as, my race is: "American," "Irish" (or some other ethnicity), "Jewish," or "Human" are not suitable replies for this exercise. Since "whiteness" is often unacknowledged in United States society, and in the rare instances where it is, often considered analogous to "racist" or "privileged," many Whites, including supervisees, are understandably reticent to self-identify as White. Another critical question for supervisees to explore and for supervisors to ask is: "What meaning do you and others attach to how you identify racially?" Once again, it is vital for the supervisor to skillfully and intensely shepherd this process along and encourage supervisees to dig a little more deeply beyond cursory responses such as: "I have never thought about it, I am not sure what meaning I attach to it." The overarching belief here is that as clinicians and supervisors it is hard to genuinely comprehend the significance that race plays in another person's life until there is some corresponding understanding about the role it plays in one's own life.

• During the case presentation, the supervisee is encouraged to hypothesize about how the phenomenon of race might be a contributing factor to the presenting problem and the maintenance of it, solutions that have been attempted by the client, and equally as importantly, the therapeutic process. Hypothesizing about race is not tantamount to a declaration that it is an issue. Instead, it is an acknowledgement that the clinician and supervisor consider it worthy of consideration.

Homework Assignment: *Between now and our next supervision, please read an Internet-based story about race as well as the comments that are submitted in response to it. Please prepare a brief Reaction Paper summarizing your observations, thoughts, and emotional reactions.*

Session Nine

• This session commences with the standard supervisory check-in, followed by a discussion and review of the homework assignment from the previous session. The focus of this session is devoted to an exploration of social class. In many ways, social class is just as difficult to discuss as is race. In fact, in some situations it can be even more challenging to discuss than race. Because class can be more readily concealed than skin color, it can have, at least on first glance, a certain invisible quality that lends itself to denial. The denial of class is also compounded by fallacious assertions that the United States is a classless society and/or that everyone is equal and can rise to the highest levels of the class hierarchy by merely pulling oneself up by one's bootstraps. Despite the plethora of heartwarming slogans about class-lessness and the overstated claims regarding everyone's ability to move heroically from rags to riches, our society is a rigidly class-stratified one comprising the Haves and the Have Nots. Interestingly, those on or at the top often experience shame in acknowledging their class privilege and those near or on the bottom of the class hierarchy often experience shame in acknowledging their class-subjugated positions. The shame of the privileged coupled with the shame of the subjugated makes meaningful conversations about class difficult to near impossible to transact.

• Once again it is the task of the supervisor to jump-start the conversation about class. The following questions can be quite useful in starting a conversation about class:

1. At what age did you first become aware of social class issues in the family you grew up in?
2. What messages did you receive about class in your family? Outside of your family?
3. How does the social class you were born into shape your attitudes, beliefs, and behavior today?

4. Is your class status the same as or different from the family you grew up in? How does the similarity or difference influence your relationships with family members?
5. What are the pride and shame issues connected to your current class status? What are the pride and shame issues connected to your former class status, if they were different?
6. What is a class-based emotional trigger that you currently have or had to work to overcome?

- These questions are designed to explore how social class may inform the self of therapist and highlight potential implications for therapy. As is usually the case, the final segment of the session is devoted to the discussion of clinical case material with the supervisor ensuring that the dimensions of culture are considered within the context of the broader clinical assessment.

Homework Assignment: *Please review a case that has been discussed in supervision and write a short statement generating a hypothesis regarding how you think social class could be a relevant dimension of it.*

Session Ten

- As is customary, this session starts with the supervisory check-in followed by a review of the homework assignment.

- Following a review of the homework assignment, the supervisee is expected to delve directly into the clinical case presentation facet of the supervisory process. In so doing, the supervisee is expected to integrate considerations of a wide array of cultural variables into the conceptualization of the case including but not limited to: how some or all cultural factors are connected to the presenting problem, maintenance of the problem, solutions attempted by the client(s), the therapeutic process and supervision. Thinking about a case culturally means that the clinician is open to the possibility that "culture" or any of its dimensions is a significant lens to use when conceptualizing case dynamics. It does not mean that the clinician is necessarily trying to ascertain how cultural factors may be problematic per se, but instead how they might inform the meaning making processes of client(s) and clinician.

- A major goal of this session is to further reinforce and promote the process of thinking culturally as a worldview. During this session, the supervisor also plants the seeds for the supervisee to consider the myriad of other cultural factors that may be relevant to attend to in therapy and supervision. Age, mental status, ability, language, and immigration status are just a few examples of additional socio-cultural factors that are instrumental to solidifying a clinician's ability to begin to think culturally.

- As the supervisory process continues, the supervisee will begin to examine these factors more organically, instinctively, and as a routine aspect of therapy and supervision.

- It is strongly recommended that the homework assignments continue throughout the course of the online supervision. The assignments become a means of promoting additional learning and they help to foster an element of intimacy in *distance learning*.

SUMMARY

This chapter has outlined guidelines for how supervisors can promote cultural sensitivity in online and electronic approaches to clinical supervision. The sample "curriculum" contained in the chapter is based on 10 sessions, a decision that was entirely arbitrary and intended for illustrative purposes. The sample that has been offered throughout this chapter was based on the following assumptions: 1) there is one supervisee involved in the ongoing supervision; 2) the supervisor is appropriately credentialed to conduct supervision, and is desirous of enhancing one's skillset to provide culturally sensitive supervision; and 3) the supervisor possesses pre-existing knowledge of the technical aspects of providing online and electronically-based supervision.

The content highlighted throughout the 10 sessions will vary significantly depending on a host of variables such as the developmental level of the supervisee, the supervisee's previous exposure to self of the therapist oriented supervision and cultural sensitivity, the particular pace of the supervision, how often sessions are scheduled, and the number of contracted sessions that have been negotiated. The content contained in the 10-session illustration could actually be truncated or elaborated extensively depending on the circumstances of the supervision. Once again, there is absolutely nothing sacred about the number of sessions or the designated content assigned to each session as presented in this chapter.

While the promotion of cultural sensitivity in supervision is probably best achieved through the use of experiential learning, the *Sample Curriculum* contained in this chapter can be quite effective in affording online supervisees experiences that will help further nurture their growth and development to become more culturally aware and sensitive practitioners.

11

Experiential Exercises

Kenneth V. Hardy, PhD and Toby Bobes, PhD

We believe that experiential teaching and learning is critical to promoting cultural sensitivity. The exercises in this chapter are designed to enhance cultural sensitivity by focusing upon self-reflective processes as well as awareness. These exercises will assist trainees in becoming more fluent in "cultural talk" and will enable them to recognize their "own culturally-based emotional triggers" (Hardy & Laszloffy, 1995, p. 228). The ability to recognize one's triggers and hot-button issues is critical to effectively manage discomfort and intensity during emotionally charged conversations.

These exercises may be used in individual, dyadic, and group supervision as well as in various training contexts. The following exercises are included in this chapter:

- Articulating a Personal Philosophy of Supervision
- The Knowledge and Use of Self Exercise
- Reflections on Cultural Images, Stories, and Experiences
- Identifying Subjugated and Privileged Selves
- Addressing Microaggressive Language in the Moment
- Deepening Difficult Dialogues in Supervision
- RASE: Racial Awareness Sensitivity Exercise

ARTICULATING A PERSONAL PHILOSOPHY OF SUPERVISION

Kenneth V. Hardy, PhD

Description and Purpose

We believe that supervision always involves assumptions whether implicit or explicit. It is often helpful when supervisors can make explicit the underlying assumptions that organize their approach to supervision. Articulation of one's personal philosophy and model of supervision is a critical first step for supervisors in developing a framework for promoting and integrating cultural sensitivity into the core of their work. This exercise is designed to facilitate this process.

Invitation

This exercise is conducted with a group of supervisors. Each supervisor is invited to articulate his or her philosophy of supervision in writing. The supervisors are asked to submit two copies of their papers, one to the trainer with their names, and the other without their names, is distributed to each group member.

Group members will read their colleagues' papers and provide feedback using the following criteria:

- Identify three strengths that are embedded in the philosophy statement.
- Pose three questions you have about the philosophy.
- What are the similarities and differences between the philosophy you are reading and your own philosophy?
- How does the philosophy reflect relational thinking?
- How does the philosophy reflect cultural/contextual thinking?
- To what extent does the supervisor's philosophy of supervision involve the supervisor's use of self and the therapist's use of self?

Discussion

For beginning supervisors, it may be helpful to suggest the exercise as a homework assignment to provide additional time for self-reflection. This would be followed by the group process described above. For more experienced supervisors this exercise might be suggested in the moment without preparation.

When supervisors turn in their papers to the trainer for feedback, an invitation for further dialogue becomes possible. This exercise adds a rich dimension of experience for the individual as well as the entire group.

THE KNOWLEDGE AND USE OF SELF EXERCISE

Kenneth V. Hardy, PhD and Toby Bobes, PhD

Description and Purpose

This exercise is designed to encourage participants to share their experiences of mistreatment. A central goal of the exercise is to emphasize the significance of stories and storytelling in promoting cultural awareness and sensitivity. Because of the powerful nature of these stories, it is important that facilitators affirm and validate each person's experience and allow ample time for processing. An essential part of the exercise is for the group to explore possibilities for future action that would address mistreatment.

Facilitation of Exercise

The facilitator invites participation by asking the following questions:

- Think of a time when you were mistreated, treated as less than or less than equal to someone else.
- Who was there?
- What happened?
- What would you have wanted to happen?
- Think of a time when you observed someone else being mistreated, treated as less than or less than equal.
- What happened?
- What did you do?
- What would you have wanted to do? (It is important to make this dialogue safe and acceptable as we cannot take actions in all situations.)

General Discussion

Participants are invited to discuss their experiences of this exercise and what they learned about themselves. They are asked to reflect upon (1) how their experience and what they learned may apply to their supervision practices, and (2) how their experience may impact their future commitment to social justice.

This exercise was adapted from material in "Visioning Social Justice: Narratives of Diversity, Social Location, and Personal Compassion" (Mock, 2008).

REFERENCE

Mock, M. R. (2008). Visioning Social Justice: Narratives of Diversity, Social Location, and Personal Compassion. In M. McGoldrick & K. V. Hardy (Eds.), *Re-visioning Family Therapy: Race, Culture, and Gender in Clinical Practice* (2nd ed.), (pp. 425–441). New York, NY: Guilford Press.

REFLECTIONS ON CULTURAL IMAGES, STORIES, AND EXPERIENCES

J. Leonardo de la O, MA

Description and Purpose

The goals of this exercise are to provide participants with the opportunity to reflect on cultural images, stories, and experiences. This activity is designed to (1) encourage participants to share cultural images, stories, and experiences in order to highlight the relevancy of culture in their lives, (2) promote cultural awareness and sensitivity, and (3) deepen empathy and promote understanding in working with people of different cultural backgrounds.

Invitation

The facilitator asks participants to bring to mind a cultural image, story, and/or cultural experience. It is important for the facilitator to model by sharing a cultural image, story, and/or cultural experience and the personal significance and meaning of this in his or her life.

Partner Sharing

In dyads, one person takes on the role of listener and the other person is the speaker. The role of the listener is simply that, to listen silently without interruption. The speaker has five minutes to talk about a cultural image, story, or experience and relate the personal meaning and significance of this to his or her life. After five minutes, the listener briefly acknowledges the speaker's story without providing interpretation.

Participants switch roles and are given equal time to discuss their image, story, or experience. This process is repeated.

The time limit should be determined by the facilitator as part of his or her time management. If this exercise is done in clinical supervision or in a classroom setting, sufficient time should be allowed for the activity and group processing.

Group Processing

After the partner sharing, the entire group processes the experience. This is an opportunity for participants to continue the conversation to talk about what the experience was like for them as both speaker and listener. An important part of this process is that each person's experience is validated by the facilitator and/or group.

The following questions may be useful:

- What did you learn about yourself as you reflect upon this experience?
- In what ways does this experience have applicability to your supervision practices?

IDENTIFYING SUBJUGATED AND PRIVILEGED SELVES

Kenneth V. Hardy, PhD

Description and Purpose

Our multiple selves are either valued (privileged) or devalued (subjugated) in the broader society. As we begin to see ourselves through the lens of our multiple selves including those that are privileged and subjugated, we are much better equipped to see others similarly. The more comprehensively we can see ourselves and others, the greater the degree of compassion, understanding, and humility we can have for each other (Hardy, 2016). This exercise is designed to (1) encourage participants to develop a more complex understanding of the self, (2) promote cultural sensitivity and awareness in working with people of different cultural backgrounds, and (3) assist supervisors to understand the role that their biases (unconscious and otherwise) may have on therapy and supervision.

Facilitation of Exercise

The facilitator invites participants to identify a subjugated self and a privileged self and to share their experiences. The facilitator shares his or her experience first.

- Identify a subjugated self and how it might appear in supervision and/or impact your role/function as a supervisor.
- Identify a privileged self and how it could appear without your knowing it.

Discussion

Supervisors are invited to discuss their experiences and what they learned about themselves. They are asked to reflect upon how their experiences and what they learned may apply to their supervision practices.

REFERENCE

Hardy, K. V. (2016). Toward the Development of a Multicultural Perspective. In K. V. Hardy & T. Bobes (Eds.), *Culturally Sensitive Supervision and Training: Diverse Perspectives and Practical Applications* (pp. 3–10). New York, NY: Routledge.

ADDRESSING MICROAGGRESSIVE LANGUAGE IN THE MOMENT

Toby Bobes, PhD

Description and Purpose

Supervisors and trainers have the responsibility to recognize and address microaggressive language when it occurs.[1] Microaggressions and oppression are perpetuated when supervisors and trainers fail to recognize and intervene by challenging insensitive remarks. The purpose of this exercise is to (1) assist supervisors, trainers, and trainees to consider the pervasive impact of microaggressions upon interactions in therapy and supervision, (2) increase awareness of unconscious bias that underlies language choice, (3) identify how *oppression operates in the concrete, everyday world of* language,[2] and (4) enhance cultural sensitivity and validate the lived experiences of our trainees.

Guidelines for Addressing Microaggressive Language

1. To address microaggressive language,[3] the supervisor must first recognize it.
2. When microaggressive language occurs, the supervisor asks the trainee about the meaning of the words used, "I am curious what you mean when you say _____." I often add, "Clarifying what we mean by words and phrases is essential so that we understand how our choice of language may impact conversations in therapy and supervision."
3. The supervisor invites other trainees to respond with their ideas about how language informs therapy and supervision conversations.

4.   The supervisor asks trainees to clarify their intentions and the possible effects of language choice. Trainees are asked to explore unintentional bias that may underlie language choice.

As a supervisor, how would you respond to the following brief scenarios?

•   A therapist describes a female client during an intake session who disclosed that she has been in her current relationship for one year. The therapist asks about how the client's relationship is going with her boyfriend.
•   A White therapist states that too much time is being spent in supervision emphasizing people's differences. She or he asserts, "I don't understand how this discussion about differences is relevant to clients' presenting problems."
•   A supervisee has a noticeable limp in his gait, and when moving about, at times, his facial expressions reflect discomfort. This supervision group of six has been meeting for six months, and the supervisor and/or group members have not yet inquired about or acknowledged his difficulty walking.
•   A White male therapist refers to his female client as a "White chick." When asked to address how he came to use this phrase, "White chick," he appeared embarrassed and at a loss for words.
•   An African American man tells his White therapist about his being passed over for promotion in a mostly White corporation. He is visibly angry and shaken by his boss's recent decision especially since he has seniority with years of service. The White therapist is taken aback when the supervisor asks him if he thinks race may have played a part in what happened to his client at work.[4]

NOTES

1   Psychiatrist and Harvard University professor Chester M. Pierce coined the word microaggression in 1970 to describe insults and dismissals he said he had regularly witnessed non-black Americans inflict on black people. In 1973, MIT economist Mary Rowe extended the term to include similar aggressions directed at women; eventually, the term came to encompass the casual degradation of any socially marginalized group, such as poor people, disabled people, and sexual minorities (Wikipedia).
2   Dee Watts Jones writes about how "oppression operates in the concrete, everyday world of language" (2004).
3   The reader is referred to the discussion about "defining, recognizing, and deconstructing hidden messages in microaggressions" (Sue, 2010).
4   The fifth scenario is drawn from the vignette of *Harold and Jeanette* (Bobes & Bobes, 2005).

REFERENCES

Bobes, T., & Bobes, N. (2005). *The Couple is Telling You What You Need to Know: Couple-Directed Therapy in a Multicultural Context.* New York, NY: Norton.
Pierce, C. M. (n.d.). In *Wikipedia.* Retrieved August 28, 2016, from https://en.wikipedia.org/wiki/Micro aggression_theory.

Rowe, M. (n.d.). In *Wikipedia*. Retrieved August 28, 2016, from https://en.wikipedia.org/wiki/Microaggres sion_theory.

Sue, D. W. (2010). *Microaggressions in Everyday Life: Race, Gender, and Sexual Orientation.* Hoboken, NJ: Wiley.

Watts Jones, D. (2004, March/April). Social Justice or Political Correctness: Confronting Racist Language in the Consulting Room. *Psychotherapy Networker, 28*(2), 27–28.

DEEPENING DIFFICULT DIALOGUES IN SUPERVISION

Toby Bobes, PhD

Description and Purpose

Supervisors promote cultural sensitivity in supervision and therapy relationships by deepening difficult dialogues about diversity and multicultural issues. This exercise is designed to (1) illustrate the use of culturally informed questions, (2) increase sensitivity about how language informs trainees' experiences, (3) provoke critical thinking and self-reflection, and (4) increase awareness of attitudes toward difference.

The following vignette illustrates a therapist's dilemma that she presents to her weekly supervision group. The group comprises an African American supervisor, two Latin men, two White women, and one White man. Supervisors address the questions below.

———————————— VIGNETTE: Maria and Hector ————————————

A White therapist, Helen, is working with a Latino couple and describes her dilemma with a tone of urgency and frustration, "I really need help today. This is the first time I've worked with a Mexican-American couple. I'm doing fine with Maria, but I'm absolutely stonewalled by Hector. I can't even get him to have eye contact with me. He looks away from me every time I try to engage him in conversation. I've never met anyone so resistant!"[1]

——————————— * * * ———————————

Questions to consider:

*   As Helen's supervisor, what questions might you ask Helen that would enable her to deepen her experience and explore the differences between herself and the couple with whom she is working?
*   As a supervisor, how do you think your race as a White Person or Person of Color would affect your interaction with Helen and with the group?
*   As a supervisor, how do you challenge supervisees' use of language that labels, pathologizes, and/or interprets behaviors?
*   How does your view of "cultural context" inform your thinking as a supervisor?

Understanding the cultural context of behavior is a valuable conceptual skill and a core supervisor competency. It is essential that we make cultural context part of the frame in which we understand the struggles, challenges, and behaviors of ourselves and others (Mock, 2008). This is critical so that we do not label, pathologize, or interpret behaviors. This point is illuminated in the vignette just described. In subsequent supervision sessions, Helen came to understand Hector's behavior in the context of his culture rather than interpreting his lack of eye contact as "resistance." Some Latin men may experience a sense of shame when they feel their manhood is challenged by being questioned. Cultural sensitivity is enhanced as we focus upon the meanings that our clients and supervisees ascribe to their behaviors rather than being limited by our particular worldviews.

Group Processing

The conversation is expanded as group members are invited to share their stories and personal experiences about difference related to gender, race, class, sexual orientation, ethnicity, and so on. The supervisor promotes *a culture of curiosity* as supervisees increase awareness of their attitudes toward difference and embrace a stance of humility and compassion (Smith, 2011, p. 61). They reflect upon how their personal experiences may inform their clinical work.

NOTE

1   The story of Hector, Maria, their children, and their therapist, Helen, are drawn from Chapter 5, "A Couple in Cultural Transition" in *The Couple is Telling You What You Need to Know: Couple-Directed Therapy in a Multicultural Context*, Bobes & Bobes, 2005. New York, NY: Norton.

REFERENCES

Bobes, T., & Bobes, N. (2005). *The Couple is Telling You What You Need to Know: Couple-Directed Therapy in a Multicultural Context*. New York, NY: Norton.

Mock, M. R. (2008). Visioning Social Justice: Narratives of Diversity, Social Location, and Personal Compassion. In M. McGoldrick & K. Hardy (Eds.), *Re-Visioning Family Therapy: Race, Culture, and Gender in Clinical Practice* (2nd ed.) (pp. 425–441). New York, NY: Guilford Press.

Smith, G. (2011). Cut the Crap: Language—Risks and Relationships in Systemic Therapy and Supervision: *The Australian and New Zealand Journal of Family Therapy*, *32*(1), 58–69.

RASE: RACIAL AWARENESS SENSITIVITY EXERCISE

Kenneth V. Hardy, PhD

Description and Purpose

The Racial Awareness and Sensitivity Exercise (RASE) is a tool designed to promote: 1) racial self-exploration and self-interrogation; 2) conversations about race; and 3) racial awareness and racial sensitivity. The tool consists of 45 race-centric semi-open-ended statements and questions that participants are invited to answer and openly share with other participants.

THE RACIAL AWARENESS AND SENSITIVITY EXERCISE

1. At what point, age, or stage of life did you begin to think of yourself racially?
2. If you had the opportunity to revisit and/or undo one significant race-related experience in your life what would it be?
3. Please describe an experience in which race was an obstacle between you and someone with whom you had a significant attachment.
4. Please identify a "race-related" conflict, tension, or misunderstanding that remains unresolved in your life today.
5. Please identify an existing race-related internal conflict and/or tension that you have between your ideals (what you think) and the practical realities of how you live your life (what you do or how you live).
6. Introduce yourself racially and share an implicit message you received about race in your family of origin or the family you grew up in.
7. In the family you grew up in, was it the implicit or explicit messages about race that have had the most influence in your life? What were those messages?
8. Of all of the racial groups placed under the broad category of "People of Color," (e.g., African Americans, Asians, Native Americans, Latinos of Color, and Mixed Race People of Color) which one do you find it easier to discuss race with? Why?
9. What is the dominant (most frequently occurring) emotion that you have in relationship to race?
10. Describe a racial fantasy that either you currently hold or have held in the past year.
11. Whom from your extended family system, especially including ancestors, would be the most proud to learn of your participation in this exercise? What would she or he say to you?
12. Who from your extended family system, especially including ancestors, would be the most disappointed that you are participating in this experience? What would she or he say to you?
13. In the family you grew up in, what racial group was considered the demonized *Other* to be shunned or avoided?
14. Can you please give at least one example of how your racial background and/or identity has informed how you related to or interacted with someone of your race?
15. How would you describe your racial trigger?
16. What is an internalized racial belief that you intellectually reject, but have difficulty completely shunning?
17. As you anticipate today's experience and your participation in it, what is the dominant emotion that you are entering with? Is it excitement, fear, anxiety, sadness, or some other emotion or parts of all of these? Please explain.
18. Of the questions that have already been answered, which one do you believe would have been the most challenging and/or growth producing for you to answer in this group at this point of the exercise?

19. What is the question about you and race that you would hope no one would ask?

20. Can you tell us now and again at the end of the day, how would this experience be different for you if you were the only member of your racial group present?

21. Of all of the race-related stories that have been in the news during the past year, which one has had the greatest emotional impact on you? Please explain.

22. Please describe how you sometimes *walk on eggshells* regarding race.

23. What makes it difficult to discuss race with *People of Color/Whites*? (Note: The purpose of this question is to gain a cross-racial perspective. Thus, the facilitator should read the question that ensures a cross-racial perspective.)

24. Please share one of the most memorable racial memories you have and discuss how it affected your sense of self.

25. What is a personal racial belief that you had earlier in life that you no longer possess today?

26. What would your personal reactions and feelings be if your child or sibling dated, married, or partnered with an African American? Would it matter if it were dating, marrying, or partnering?

27. In the family you grew up in, who would currently be or would have been at some point the most challenging person for you to have an honest, open, and candid conversation with regarding your racial views? Why?

28. If there was one question that you could ask a *Person of Color/White Person* without fear of reprisal, backlash, offense or any other impediment to having a deeper conversation about race, what would your question be? (Note: The facilitator chooses "Person of Color" or "White" depending on the racial identity of the participant receiving the question.)

29. What does it mean to be White?

30. What is a racial stereotype or belief that you believe you have to make a concerted effort to debunk virtually every day in your interactions with peers, co-workers, or colleagues of a different race?

31. Based on your experience and/or perspective, which is the bigger problem: Whites always claiming to not see race, or People of Color always seeing race?

32. What does it mean to be a Person of Color in the United States?

33. What is a race-related memory that you have of something that a person of another race said, failed to say, did, or failed to do that was hurtful to you?

34. As you think of yourself racially, what is a racially-based trait, attribution, feature, behavior, or physical characteristic that you currently reject, had to overcome, currently struggle with, or had to work hard to accept?

35. If you could offer two recommendations to help improve race relationships, one to People of Color and one to Whites, what would your recommendations be?

36. What is a race-related memory that you have of something that a person of your race said, failed to say, did, or failed to do that was hurtful to you?

37. Please share two messages you heard about members of another racial group that you no longer believe but had to overcome.

38. Given all that you know and have experienced regarding the role that race plays in our lives, if you could start life over again and choose your race, what race would you choose to be and why?

39. Of all of the racial groups placed under the broad category of "People of Color," (e.g., African Americans, Asians, Native Americans, Latinos of Color, and Mixed Race People of Color) which one do you generally find it most challenging to discuss race with? Why?

40. What is a trait, characteristic, or feature associated with your racial group that is a source of pride for you?

41. Prior to this exercise, when was the last time you participated in a conversation about race? What was the outcome?

42. When witnessing an act of racial injustice or racism, what role do you most typically assume?

43. What is your personal cutting edge struggle or shortcoming that you have to conquer in order to be more effective in talking about race in a more progressive and productive way?

44. On a scale from 1–10 where one is hardly and 10 is constantly, how much effort would you suggest you devote to increasing your sense of racial awareness and sensitivity?

45. Can you please give at least one example of how your racial background and/or identity has informed how you related to or interacted with someone of a different race?

These questions can be adjusted and/or modified as the clinical and/or training needs of the trainer and/or trainee necessitate. They can be used in one session or across several different sessions. As noted earlier, the RASE can also be implemented in a variety of different settings.

Settings and Format

The exercise can be used in a variety of settings and formats as an effective training and/or supervisory tool for promoting intense conversations about race. One of the major objectives of the RASE is to promote conversations and for this purpose it tends to works best in settings where there are multiple participants engaged in the process and where interpersonal interaction is encouraged. Another goal of the exercise is to encourage self-exploration and self-interrogation that ideally can be achieved individually and/or collectively. The following is a brief summary of how the format of the exercise can be implemented in different settings:

• **Individual Supervision**: In one-on-one supervision the exercise can be used as a type of icebreaker before the beginning of supervision or as a closure exercise implemented towards the end of supervision session. In any event, the supervisor commences the process by providing the supervisee with background information about the exercise, including a statement about its goals and objectives. The supervisor then provides a quick overview of the *rules of engagement* for participating in the exercise. The supervisor might define the rules in one of the following ways: a) the supervisee will be asked to select a question between 1–30 and provide an answer that best reflects their thoughts, beliefs, and/or experiences. The supervisor then must be willing to answer the same question. Once the item has been addressed by supervisor and supervisee, the former initiates a discussion regarding implications for both the self of the therapist and the process of therapy; or b) instead of the supervisor answering/addressing the same item, the supervisee is asked to pick another number between 1–45 and this time the supervisor is expected to address the selected item. Regardless of the format, the actual discussion of thoughts, feelings, and reflections about the questions should be reserved until both parties have had the opportunity to address at least one item from the RASE. Depending on the philosophical orientation of the supervisor, she or he may prefer *not* to address an item, which is certainly a matter of personal choice.

- **Dyadic Supervision**: In supervision where there are two supervisees present with a supervisor, the execution of the RASE in many ways, may replicate the process described under Individual Supervision with a few variations. Following the overview of the exercise, the supervisor then asks each supervisee to select a number between 1–45 and they cannot select the same number. It is important that Supervisee 2 does not select a number until after Supervisee 1 has fully addressed the item that she or he selected. When both supervisees select their respective numbers at the same time, it can be a mild distraction because Supervisee 2 is often thinking about his or her question and answer rather than devoting full attention to Supervisee 1. If the supervisor chooses to participate at this level, as in the case with individual supervision, she or he might ask Supervisee 1 to select a number between 1–45 for the supervisor to address. Supervisee 1 is usually afforded *the privilege* of selecting the supervisor's number as a "reward" for volunteering to go first. Alternatively, the supervisor may assign the task of picking the supervisor's number on a rotating basis.

- **Group Supervision**: The overall process for group supervision replicates that of dyadic supervision. Unlike individual and dyadic supervision approaches, there are exceedingly more dynamics for the supervisor to attend to from moment to moment. The larger the group, the more items that will be introduced into the process. With every question that is asked and ultimately addressed, there tends to be an *accumulative effect* that emerges which usually increases the intensity of the group. In one sense it is the power of the group dynamic that is in play. It is commonplace for a group supervision supervisee to privately muse about how she or he would have answered all of the questions that precedes one's personal selection of a number. The role of the supervisor/facilitator (which will be discussed later) is critical to the effective execution of the exercise.

- **Large Class/Training Settings**: The exercise can be used with classes and/or training groups of virtually any size, with some modifications. In groups of 45 participants, there is one question for each member to address. Once again, it is best to delay any general group-wide discussion of the questions until after each participant has had the opportunity to receive and address an item, unless there is some extenuating circumstance requiring a departure from this general guideline. In groups over 45, it may be necessary for more than one participant to address the same item. For example, Participant A volunteers and choses item 23. Once she or he has fully addressed the issue, Participant A is then asked to choose someone from the group to address the same item. The facilitator, for instance, may or may not give additional instructions to Participant A, such as, "Can you select someone whom you assume is of a different race to address the same item?" Once Participant B responds, she or he is then asked to choose someone from the group based on some random criterion (e.g., someone you would like to know better). The number of participants assigned to the same item would ultimately be determined by the size of the group. In all of the settings, it is imperative for the facilitator to be acutely attentive to body language, nonverbal gestures, as well as the verbal disclosures shared by the participants. Obviously, this task becomes increasingly more challenging as the number of participants increases.

Role of the Facilitator and General Guidelines for Execution

Whether a supervisor or trainer, the role assumed and executed by the facilitator is central to the overall success for the exercise. It is critical that the facilitator has been actively engaged in a process of self-interrogation and self-exploration regarding one's racial identity, location, and background prior to implementing the exercise. The exercise often triggers intense emotions and the facilitator must be able to effectively tolerate and respond to intense emotions while using oneself to cultivate an environment of safety and relational risk-taking. Accordingly, it is crucial that the facilitator assists the participants in drawing the critical distinction between *safety and comfort*. Thus, it is possible to feel intense discomfort without the feeling undermining or compromising safety. The facilitator must be *comfortable with discomfort* in order for the important developmental step in the process of conversing and engaging about race to be effectively implemented.

Given that most racially based conversations in society are mired in discomfort, most attempts to integrate racial discussions in supervision and training are no exception. Consequently, so much of our deeply rooted feelings about race are often masked by silence, expressed in innuendo and highly coded language, or unconsciously expressed through a myriad of non-verbal cues and communication. The facilitator of the RASE must be attuned to these *particular peculiarities* associated with promoting racial conversations and engagement. Thus, the facilitator must be skilled and poised enough to strike the appropriate and delicate balance between active engagement and appropriate detachment. On the one hand the facilitator must be engaged enough to attend to the micro-level interactions that will occur between individual members, self-disclose when it is needed to further augment the interactional processes, as well as remain *detached* enough that she or he can maintain an "aerial view" of the entire process. When the facilitator is too intimately embedded in the micro-level processes, it becomes virtually impossible to acknowledge and/or respond to the host of other more subtle reactions that might be occurring in response to the exercise. On the other hand, the reverse is also true, when the facilitator focuses too narrowly on the macro level processes with a sense of oblivion to the dynamics that may be occurring between specific individuals. A major key to the effective implementation of the RASE rests with the facilitator having a good intuitive sense about when to *lean into* the process (i.e., increase engagement) and when to *pull back*. As a general guideline it is important for the facilitator to lean in or engage to increase interaction, intensity, and vulnerability or to defuse or de-escalate nascent conflicts that are void of vulnerability or threaten the overall process. Consider the following vignette.

———————————— VIGNETTE: **The Case of Whiteness** ————————————

The RASE was employed in a group supervision session with eight supervisees participating. Nicole, a White female member of the group and the third supervisee to choose an item, chose #29, "What does it mean to be White?" Her face immediately flushed as she began to fidget. She sat silently with a slight incongruent smile on her face for several seconds. The more time that elapsed, the greater the discomfort and intensity increased throughout the room. After several prolonged sighs and aborted utterances, she said, as if speaking to herself: "Hmm, what does it mean to be White." The longer she paused and contemplated her reply, the more agitated several supervisees of color in the group became. Finally, Naveen, a South-Asian male could no longer tolerate Nicole's silence or reticence to say what she thought it meant to be White. In total frustration, he interrupted and began interjecting. "What is this some kind of a joke? Do you want us to sit here and believe that YOU DON'T KNOW WHAT THE HELL IT MEANS TO BE WHITE?" At this point, Nicole began to shut down even more. The facilitator intervened initially by acknowledging and validating Naveen's passion and impatience, and then by reminding him that there would be ample time allocated for discussion after everyone had an opportunity to select an item. He was subsequently asked to grant Nicole the emotional space to think through her answer and to also spend some time exploring both the depth and anatomy of his reactions to Nicole's silence. The facilitator also addressed Nicole directly and acknowledged and validated her struggle with the question as well as her resolve to find an answer that was acceptable to her. After squirming for a while longer, Nicole eventually stated, somewhat hesitantly: "I think being White means . . . being blamed for everything." The supervisees of color silently responded with fury-laced disbelief while many of the White supervisees appeared puzzled. Naveen, who was obviously frustrated, began steadily tapping the right arm of his chair with his fingers while his left foot loudly and seemingly unconsciously tapped the floor in a consistent and rhythmic fashion. The facilitator asked Chauncey, an African male supervisee, who appeared physically agitated and annoyed, if he would share his thoughts and feelings with the group. He responded with a degree of feigned animation, perhaps attempting to disguise his authentic feelings, by laughing and stating: "Wow, this is all really deep! If I had that question, damn . . . I could take all day answering it!" The facilitator then asked him: "Why? What would you say?" He repeated:

What does it mean to be White? Well I will tell you what it means to be White. Being White means stepping on and over people and never having to say you are sorry. Being White means choosing to not see or acknowledge People of Color on a daily basis no matter what relationship you have with them. Being White means walking around like you are superior and everyone else around you are less than you. Being White means to believe it is your God-given birthright to define other people's experience, deny their cultures and their realities. Being White means taking . . . no, stealing whatever you want from other cultures and claiming it as your own. Being White means to be a part of a group that historically and systematically oppresses the lives of non-White people and then blames them for their conditions and failures. Being White means being so spiritually and culturally broken that you don't know how broken you are or how you cope with it by destroying the lives of others with no conscience, sense of remorse, or accountability. This is what I think it means to be White!

Chauncey spoke with a sense of conviction, well-managed rage, and a great deal of pain. With unacknowledged tears slowly crawling down his face, he barely took a breath as he cited what it meant to be White in an almost poetry-like fashion. The room was completely silent, the mood was somber and reflective, and the members of the group seemed to coalesce around the individual and collective tears they were sharing.

This vignette illustrates how pivotal the role of the facilitator is to the overall effective execution of the RASE. Within the same session, it was necessary for the facilitator at one juncture, to gently ask Naveen to refrain from interrupting Nicole and to defer his comments until later in the process and then a few minutes later, invite Chauncey to participate before he and other group members had the opportunity to select a question. Although the facilitator's actions may appear arbitrary at first glance, they were actually well conceived and perfectly timed. Naveen was asked to refrain from speaking at the time because the more he spoke, the more disengaged Nicole would have become from the group process. Also, her obvious struggle with the question was increasing the intensity in the group and both she and the group would have welcomed the emotional distraction and "escape" that Naveen's ill-timed feedback was guaranteed to provide. Chauncey, on the other hand, was asked a few minutes later to answer Nicole's question from his perspective. This request was made as a means to maintain the intensity of the group but also to potentially (and hopefully) increase intimacy (vulnerability). Both the decision to defer Naveen's comments and to solicit Chauncey's was a judgment call made by the facilitator based on the interactional dynamics of the group at a given moment.

———————————— * * * ————————————

Sample Group Processing Questions*

Once all participants have had the opportunity to select and address an item, the next important step is to have a facilitated all-participant discussion about the exercise. A major goal of the facilitated discussion is to create an opportunity for all participants to explore and share with each other the range of thoughts, feelings, reflections, and epiphanies (if any) that were inspired by the RASE. The following is a list of sample questions that may be used to initiate the post exercise discussion and processing.

1. What recurring thoughts did you have about the unfolding of this exercise and your emerging role in it?
2. What feelings did the exercise generate for you?
3. Which group member had the question that you were relieved that you didn't select? Why? How would you have answered it?
4. Which group member had the question that you wished you had received? Why? How would you have answered it?
5. Who within the group did you have the greatest compassion for based on either the question selected or the answer given?

6. Of all of the answers you heard, which one bothered you the most? Why?
7. Of all of the answers you heard, which one left you feeling the most hopeful about race and race relationships?
8. What did you learn about yourself as a result of participating in this exercise?
9. On a scale from 1–10, with 1 representing a total lack of honesty and 10 denoting total honesty, how would you rate your level of honesty in answering your question and throughout this exercise?
10. What are your preliminary thoughts about how your participation in this exercise will impact your work as a therapist, as well as your life as a citizen of the planet?
11. If you received a metaphorical gift from participating in this exercise, what was it and can you take a moment to express your gratitude to the member(s) who bestowed it upon you?

Note:

* These questions have been designed for groups but can be easily modified for individual and dyadic experiences.

Exercise Summary

The RASE is a tool that can be used to foster conversations about race while simultaneously promoting racial awareness and sensitivity. It is predicated on the notion that the more "practice" each of us has in talking about race, the less awkward and easier it becomes for us to do so. It is also designed to promote racial self-reflection and interrogation, which are potent precursors to enhancing racial awareness and sensitivity—the backbone of increased racial understanding. Without some development and refinement of racial awareness and sensitivity, racial conversations continue to range from guarded, sterile, and polarized to explosive and non-productive. There is tremendous healing and transformative potential embedded in conversation and dialogue. Thus, the more we, as a society, can risk engaging with each other in difficult conversations about race the bigger the strides we take in bridging the racial gulf that not only divides us but places our shared humanity at considerable and perpetual risk.

CONCLUDING REMARKS

Experiential teaching and learning is an integral component of fostering cultural awareness and sensitivity. The exercises contained in this chapter are designed towards this specific goal. They can be adjusted and applied to a variety of supervision modalities and configurations. The exercises, when used properly, can also be effective in assisting supervisors and supervisees develop facility and proficiency with discussing diversity-related topics that may otherwise engender awkwardness and discomfort when discussed without preparation and/or experience.

REFERENCE

Hardy, K. V., & Laszloffy, T. A. (1995). The Cultural Genogram: Key to Training Culturally Competent Family Therapists. *Journal of Marital and Family Therapy, 21*(3), 227–237.

Part IV

EVALUATION TOOLS

12

The Multicultural Relational Perspective

Supervision Outcome Tools for Mental Health Professionals

Kenneth V. Hardy, PhD

INTRODUCTION

The Multicultural Relational Perspective Supervision Outcome Tools are designed to evaluate the knowledge, skills, commitment, and qualities of supervisors and supervisees toward the goal of enhancing the effectiveness of both supervision and clinical practice from a multicultural relational perspective. From the multicultural relational perspective, self-reflection and self-interrogation are critical components of effective supervision and clinical practice. The measures included in the tools provide an opportunity for supervisors and supervisees to consider/assess their multicultural knowledge, knowledge of self and self in relation to other, commitment/motivational skills, administrative/training skills and/or competency. Specifically, the sections of measure focus on the assessment of supervision/practice from the perspective of the supervisor/supervisee, the supervisory/therapeutic relationship/process, evaluation of supervision and the supervisor's/therapist's style of supervision/therapy. Each of the sections includes a brief introduction and scoring instructions. Definitions of selected key terms of the Multicultural Relational Perspective may be found at the end of this chapter.

SUPERVISOR SELF-ASSESSMENT

Self-Assessment of Supervisor Competencies

The following measure is to provide an opportunity for you to reflect on and assess your current level of perceived knowledge, skill and commitment as a supervisor from the Multicultural Relational Perspective. Please rate your level of competence using the following scale with lower scores revealing needed learning and skill development.

1	2	3	4	5
Learning		*Competent*		*Expert*

Knowledge

Understand the purpose of the Multicultural Relational Perspective.	1	2	3	4	5
Knowledge of multiculturalism.	1	2	3	4	5
Understand that human suffering is located within relationships.	1	2	3	4	5
Knowledge of the relational context.	1	2	3	4	5
Knowledge of family systems theory.	1	2	3	4	5
Clear about differences due to: race, ethnicity, culture, gender, class, religion/spirituality, sexual orientation, age, and ability.	1	2	3	4	5
Clear about differences in power and privilege due to: race, ethnicity, culture, gender, class, religion/spirituality, sexual orientation, age, and ability.	1	2	3	4	5
Understand the hidden wounds and trauma of oppression.	1	2	3	4	5
Understand the importance of a structured approach to talking about race.	1	2	3	4	5
Understand the systemic or relational nature of supervision.	1	2	3	4	5
Understand own social locations in relation to supervisee's social locations.	1	2	3	4	5
Can acknowledge power and privilege in the supervisory . relationship	1	2	3	4	5
Understand the importance of responsibility and accountability in establishing mutual trust and reciprocity.	1	2	3	4	5

Supervisor Management Skills

Can explain to supervisees the purpose of the Multicultural Relational Perspective.	1	2	3	4	5
Can explain to supervisees the relational context.	1	2	3	4	5
Can negotiate a clear and mutually agreed upon supervision contract.	1	2	3	4	5
Can maintain appropriate boundaries.	1	2	3	4	5
Can use self-disclosure appropriately to foster supervisee's growth and skill development.	1	2	3	4	5
Can address power and privilege and the myth of equality in the supervisory relationship.	1	2	3	4	5
Can facilitate a meaningful conversation about race.	1	2	3	4	5
Can set a supervision climate that is conducive to questioning and examining socio-cultural factors and relationship issues between the supervisor and supervisee.	1	2	3	4	5
Can avoid using my racial self to make meaning for others.	1	2	3	4	5
Can demonstrate comfort, humility and sensitivity with respect to differences due to: race, ethnicity, culture, gender, class, sexual orientation, religion/spirituality, immigration status, age, and ability.	1	2	3	4	5
Can recognize and manage emotional triggers based on contextual variables (e.g., race, ethnicity, gender, class, etc.).	1	2	3	4	5

Supervisor Intervention Skills

Can describe and demonstrate own philosophy of supervision.	1	2	3	4	5
Can explain and demonstrate own theory of change.	1	2	3	4	5
Can use power and authority inherent in the supervisor's role to create space for talking about race and other contextual variables.	1	2	3	4	5
Can encourage, motivate, and engage in intense racial and other contextually related conversations.	1	2	3	4	5
Can identify and track relational processes in supervision.	1	2	3	4	5
Can use validation and challenging effectively to address supervisee's conscious and unconscious biases due to contextual variables.	1	2	3	4	5
Can communicate using "I" messages.	1	2	3	4	5
Can provide feedback that is clear, owned, and contextualized.	1	2	3	4	5
Can address differences between self and supervisee due to contextual variables.	1	2	3	4	5

Can demonstrate acceptance of subjugated or oppressed groups' knowledge and experiences.	1	2	3	4	5
Can use the Multicultural Relational Perspective for resolving impasses due to contextual variables.	1	2	3	4	5
Can facilitate supervisee's work on self of the therapist issues.	1	2	3	4	5
Can motivate supervisee's self-reflection and self-interrogation.	1	2	3	4	5
Can do own work on self of the supervisor issues.	1	2	3	4	5

Self of the Supervisor

Awareness of multiple identities or multiple selves.	1	2	3	4	5
Awareness and sensitivity to subjugated and privileged selves.	1	2	3	4	5
Awareness and knowledge of own family of origin and cultural context.	1	2	3	4	5
Recognition of own cultural pride and shame.	1	2	3	4	5
Proactive identification and management of self of the supervisor issues or emotional triggers.	1	2	3	4	5
Comfortable with being vulnerable and taking risks.	1	2	3	4	5
Sensitive to supervisee's person of the therapist issues.	1	2	3	4	5

Supervisor Commitment

Consider race a powerful organizing principle in life.	1	2	3	4	5
Recognize the centrality of relationships.	1	2	3	4	5
Committed to creating space to talk about race and other contextual variables.	1	2	3	4	5
Committed to remaining connected in intense race conversations.	1	2	3	4	5
Committed to own and supervisee's self-reflection and self-interrogation.	1	2	3	4	5
Embrace a "Both/And" philosophy.	1	2	3	4	5
Committed to seeking and being open to ongoing feedback.	1	2	3	4	5
Recognize degree of responsibility and accountability is proportional to power and privilege.	1	2	3	4	5
Acknowledge distinction between intentions and consequences.	1	2	3	4	5
Avoid minimizing, re-interpreting, correcting, marginalizing, lecturing, or negating supervisee's cultural worldview.	1	2	3	4	5
Avoid neutral, objective, all-knowing expert stance.	1	2	3	4	5
Hold on to commitment when in doubt.	1	2	3	4	5

SUPERVISOR-SUPERVISEE EVALUATION OF SUPERVISION

Evaluation of Supervision

The following measure is designed to assess your experience of the quality of supervision from the Multicultural Relational Perspective. Please rate your level of experience using the rating scale below.

1	2	3	4
Almost Never	Occasionally	Often	Almost Always

Quality of the Supervisory Process	*Supervisor/ Supervisee*			
1. The supervisor/supervisee negotiated a mutually agreed upon contract.	1	2	3	4
2. The supervisor/supervisee maintains appropriate boundaries.	1	2	3	4
3. The supervisor/supervisee creates an environment of mutual trust.	1	2	3	4
4. The supervisor/supervisee utilizes the Multicultural Relational Perspective.	1	2	3	4
5. The supervisor/supervisee uses a trauma-informed lens.	1	2	3	4
6. The supervisor/supervisee appropriately uses self to connect.	1	2	3	4
7. The supervisor/supervisee uses self-disclosure appropriately to foster growth and change.	1	2	3	4
8. The supervisor/supervisee attends to differences due to contextual variables.	1	2	3	4
9. The supervisor/supervisee places a high priority on power and privilege based on contextual variables.	1	2	3	4
10. The supervisor/supervisee engages in open, honest racial and other contextual conversations.	1	2	3	4
11. The supervisor/supervisee considers own race and other's race.	1	2	3	4
12. The supervisor/supervisee does not use racial self to make meaning for other.	1	2	3	4
13. The supervisor/supervisee uses authority inherent in role to create space for talking about race and other contextual variables.	1	2	3	4
14. The supervisor/supervisee uses a structured approach to talking about race.	1	2	3	4
15. The supervisor/supervisee uses validation and challenging effectively.	1	2	3	4

16.	The supervisor/supervisee encourages self-reflection and self-interrogation of biases.	1	2	3	4

16. The supervisor/supervisee encourages self-reflection and self-interrogation of biases. 1 2 3 4

17. The supervisor/supervisee does own work. 1 2 3 4

18. The supervisor/supervisee demonstrates enthusiasm and commitment to professional development and growth. 1 2 3 4

19. The supervisor/supervisee maintains a stance of cultural curiosity and humility. 1 2 3 4

20. The supervisor/supervisee accepts responsibility and accountability for intended and unintended consequences. 1 2 3 4

21. The supervisor/supervisee communicates using "I" messages. 1 2 3 4

Outcomes of Supervision	**Supervisor/ Supervisee**			

22. Supervision enhanced supervisee's knowledge of multiculturalism and the relational context. 1 2 3 4

23. Supervision increased supervisee's awareness of and sensitivity to differences in power and privilege based on contextual variables. 1 2 3 4

24. Supervision increased supervisee's ability to use the Multicultural Relational Perspective in treatment. 1 2 3 4

25. Supervision increased supervisee's awareness of the hidden wounds of oppression and trauma. 1 2 3 4

26. Supervision increased supervisee's knowledge and understanding of person of the therapist issues. 1 2 3 4

27. Supervision increased supervisee's knowledge of subjugated and privileged selves. 1 2 3 4

28. Supervision motivated the supervisee to confront and challenge conscious and unconscious biases. 1 2 3 4

29. Supervision encouraged supervisee to be aware of and attend to differences due to: race, ethnicity, culture, gender, class, immigration status, sexual orientation, religion/spirituality, age, and ability. 1 2 3 4

30. Supervision helped the supervisee to remain connected in intense racial and other contextually related conversations. 1 2 3 4

31. Supervision helped the supervisee develop culturally congruent interventions. 1 2 3 4

32. What are the three most compelling outcomes that you achieved from this supervision?

a)

b)

c)

33. What are the three least compelling outcomes that you achieved from this supervision?

    a)

    b)

    c)

34. What additional knowledge or skills would you like to develop with the help of supervision?

35. What would you like to see added to or changed in the supervisory process?

SUPERVISION SATISFACTION BASED ON THE MULTICULTURAL RELATIONAL PERSPECTIVE TRAINING

The Multicultural Relational Perspective Supervision Satisfaction Questionnaire

---

The Multicultural Relational Perspective Supervision Satisfaction Questionnaire measures the supervisor's/supervisee's satisfaction with this particular approach to supervision and practice.

---

1. What is the quality of supervision you have received based on the Multicultural Relational Perspective training?

    ❏ Excellent   ❏ Good   ❏ Fair   ❏ Poor

2. Did training from the Multicultural Relational Perspective meet your supervision/clinical needs?

    ❏ No, Definitely Not   ❏ No, Not Really   ❏ Yes, Generally   ❏ Yes, Definitely

3. Would you recommend the Multicultural Relational Perspective to others?

    ❏ No, Definitely Not   ❏ No, I Don't Think So   ❏ Yes, I Think So   ❏ Yes, Definitely

4. Were you satisfied with the level of the Multicultural Relational Perspective training/supervision you received?

    ❏ Dissatisfied   ❏ Somewhat Dissatisfied   ❏ Somewhat Satisfied   ❏ Satisfied   ❏ Very Satisfied

5. Did the Multicultural Relational Perspective training your supervisor received help your supervisor to be more effective in the role of supervisor?

    ❏ No, Definitely Not   ❏ No, Not Really   ❏ Yes, Generally   ❏ Yes, Definitely

6. Did you feel your supervisor was prepared adequately to attend to self of the therapist's issues?

   ❏ No, Definitely Not   ❏ No, Not Really   ❏ Yes, Generally   ❏ Yes, Definitely

7. Did your supervisor attend to contextual variables in the supervisory relationship?

   ❏ No, Definitely Not   ❏ No, Not Really   ❏ Yes, Generally   ❏ Yes, Definitely

8. Did your supervisor use a trauma-informed lens?

   ❏ No, Definitely Not   ❏ No, Not Really   ❏ Yes, Generally   ❏ Yes, Definitely

9. Did your supervisor attend to the relational context?

   ❏ No, Definitely Not   ❏ No, Not Really   ❏ Yes, Generally   ❏ Yes, Definitely

10. Did your supervisor demonstrate knowledge of a family systems approach?

    ❏ No, Definitely Not   ❏ No, Not Really   ❏ Yes, Generally   ❏ Yes, Definitely

11. Did your supervisor articulate a philosophy of supervision?

    ❏ No, Definitely Not   ❏ No, Not Really   ❏ Yes, Generally   ❏ Yes, Definitely

12. Did your supervisor describe a theory of change?

    ❏ No, Definitely Not   ❏ No, Not Really   ❏ Yes, Generally   ❏ Yes, Definitely

13. Did your supervisor demonstrate a structured approach to talking about race?

    ❏ No, Definitely Not   ❏ No, Not Really   ❏ Yes, Generally   ❏ Yes, Definitely

14. Would you want your supervisor to do more training in the Multicultural Relational Perspective?

    ❏ No, Definitely Not   ❏ No, I Don't Think So   ❏ Yes, I Think So   ❏ Yes, Definitely

---

EVALUATION OF SUPERVISORY RELATIONSHIP

Supervisory Relationship Inventory

The Supervisory Relationship Inventory measures the supervisee's experience of the supervisor's qualities and skills. Please indicate your agreement using the following rating scale.

1	2	3	4	5	6	7
Strongly Disagree			*Moderately Agree*			*Strongly Agree*

1. My supervisor and I devised goals based on the Multicultural Relational Perspective.   1 2 3 4 5 6 7

2. My supervisor and I talked about our worldview based on contextual variables.   1 2 3 4 5 6 7

3. My supervisor and I discussed our differences due to contextual variables. 1 2 3 4 5 6 7

4. My supervisor and I discussed our power and privilege due to contextual variables. 1 2 3 4 5 6 7

5. My supervisor and I experienced mutual trust. 1 2 3 4 5 6 7

6. My supervisor and I shared open and honest communication. 1 2 3 4 5 6 7

7. My supervisor and I communicated using "I" messages. 1 2 3 4 5 6 7

8. My supervisor and I worked collaboratively. 1 2 3 4 5 6 7

9. My supervisor and I remained connected in intense racial and other contextually related conversations. 1 2 3 4 5 6 7

10. My supervisor and I engaged in racial conversations without defensiveness, suspicion, fear, and negative accusations. 1 2 3 4 5 6 7

11. My supervisor and I recognized race as an essential dimension of life. 1 2 3 4 5 6 7

12. My supervisor and I recognized the centrality of relationships. 1 2 3 4 5 6 7

13. My supervisor and I attended to relational processes and managed emotional triggers based on contextual variables. 1 2 3 4 5 6 7

14. My supervisor and I distinguished between intentions and consequences. 1 2 3 4 5 6 7

15. My supervisor and I took responsibility proportional to our power and privilege. 1 2 3 4 5 6 7

16. My supervisor and I risked vulnerability. 1 2 3 4 5 6 7

17. My supervisor and I used our voices confidently. 1 2 3 4 5 6 7

18. My supervisor and I practiced the skill of validating and challenging. 1 2 3 4 5 6 7

19. My supervisor and I identified self of the supervisor and self of the therapist issues. 1 2 3 4 5 6 7

20. My supervisor and I used self-disclosure to enhance effectiveness. 1 2 3 4 5 6 7

21. My supervisor and I discussed family of origin and cultural pride and shame. 1 2 3 4 5 6 7

Feedback

#		1	2	3	4	5	6	7
22.	My supervisor gave consistent clear feedback.	1	2	3	4	5	6	7
23.	My supervisor solicited my feedback on the supervisory relationship.	1	2	3	4	5	6	7
25.	My supervisor provided feedback without minimizing, marginalizing, or dismissing my worldview.	1	2	3	4	5	6	7
26.	My supervisor provided feedback on self of the therapist issues impacting therapy.	1	2	3	4	5	6	7
27.	My supervisor provided constructive feedback on use of the Multicultural Relational Perspective.	1	2	3	4	5	6	7
28.	My supervisor provided feedback on the supervisory process.	1	2	3	4	5	6	7
29.	My supervisor encouraged my feedback on relational differences due to contextual variables.	1	2	3	4	5	6	7
30.	My supervisor welcomed comments about the supervisory process and his/her philosophy of supervision.	1	2	3	4	5	6	7

SUPERVISION OUTCOMES SURVEY

The Multicultural Relational Perspective Outcomes Survey

Please answer the following questions using the below rating scale.

1	2	3	4	5	6	7
Not at All			Moderately		Greatest Degree Possible	

#		1	2	3	4	5	6	7
1.	My supervisor helps me to conceptualize my clinical cases from the Multicultural Relational Perspective.	1	2	3	4	5	6	7
2.	The Multicultural Relational Perspective helps me to think relationally.	1	2	3	4	5	6	7
3.	The Multicultural Relational Perspective helps me to think culturally.	1	2	3	4	5	6	7
4.	The Multicultural Relational Perspective helps me use a trauma-informed lens in clinical practice.	1	2	3	4	5	6	7

5. The Multicultural Relational Perspective helps me to be aware of and attend to client differences due to contextual variables. 1 2 3 4 5 6 7

6. The Multicultural Relational Perspective helps me to be aware of and attend to power and privilege based on contextual variables. 1 2 3 4 5 6 7

7. The Multicultural Relational Perspective helps me to recognize and manage self of the therapist issues. 1 2 3 4 5 6 7

8. The Multicultural Relational Perspective helps me to understand my responsibility as the therapist to address race. 1 2 3 4 5 6 7

9. The Multicultural Relational Perspective provides me a structured approach to talking about race. 1 2 3 4 5 6 7

10. The Multicultural Relational Perspective prepares me to facilitate a more meaningful conversation about race. 1 2 3 4 5 6 7

11. The Multicultural Relational Perspective helps me to better understand my own family of origin and cultural context. 1 2 3 4 5 6 7

12. The Multicultural Relational Perspective helps me to be aware of and attend to my own cultural pride and shame. 1 2 3 4 5 6 7

13. The Multicultural Relational Perspective helps me to distinguish between intentions and consequences and be accountable for consequences. 1 2 3 4 5 6 7

14. The Multicultural Relational Perspective helps me to be aware of and manage emotional triggers due to contextual variables. 1 2 3 4 5 6 7

15. The Multicultural Relational Perspective is better preparing me to remain engaged in intense racial conversations. 1 2 3 4 5 6 7

16. The Multicultural Relational Perspective better helps me to use validating and challenging as strategies. 1 2 3 4 5 6 7

17. My supervisor recognizes issues of power and privilege based on our different social locations. 1 2 3 4 5 6 7

18. Awareness of self of the therapist helps me to better connect to clients. 1 2 3 4 5 6 7

19. Awareness of privileged and subjugated selves helps me to avoid speaking from an all-knowing position. 1 2 3 4 5 6 7

20. My supervisor's awareness of self of the supervisor helps me to be more open and trusting. 1 2 3 4 5 6 7

21. My supervisor's willingness to acknowledge contextual variables helps me to talk more openly with my clients about contextual variables. 1 2 3 4 5 6 7

22. My supervisor's ability to manage emotional reactivity helps to lower my defenses, fear and negative reactions. 1 2 3 4 5 6 7

23. My supervisor acknowledges the power and authority inherent in the role of supervisor and creates space to attend to contextual variables. 1 2 3 4 5 6 7

24. My supervisor's work on self motivates me to do my own work. 1 2 3 4 5 6 7

25. Overall, I feel the Multicultural Relational Perspective training/supervision is enhancing my clinical effectiveness with diverse clients. 1 2 3 4 5 6 7

The outcome tools presented in this chapter are built upon the Multicultural Relational Perspective. Evaluation tools are most effective when there is a goodness of fit between the supervisor's philosophy of supervision and the measures of assessment. In a sense, outcome tools are like a curriculum. The evaluation process is enhanced when there is a coherence between the curriculum and the evaluation tool.

DEFINITIONS OF SELECTED KEY TERMS OF THE MULTICULTURAL RELATIONAL PERSPECTIVE

Contextual denotes various social locations, such as race, ethnicity, culture, gender, class, religion/spirituality, sexual orientation, geography, immigration status, age, and ability.

Family Oriented refers to a systems view of individual development within the context of family development.

Multicultural Relational Perspective is premised on the belief that therapy and supervision are parallel processes based on the following key principles: a) the centrality of relationships and the notion that human suffering occurs within the context of relationships; b) that cultural factors are salient contextual variables in our lives and must be attended to with humility, sensitivity, and competence; c) that an understanding of socio-cultural trauma and the hidden wounds associated with it are essential to clinical effectiveness; and d) that an acute exploration of the self of the supervisor and self of the therapist are critical to the effective practice of supervision and therapy.

Muticulturalism is awareness of the co-existence of different ways of knowing, thinking, believing, and behaving based on factors including but not limited to race, ethnicity, religion, and country of origin.

Multidimensional Selves refers to the various social components of an individual's identity based on race, class, gender, sexual orientation, religion/spirituality, etc.

Power refers to the possession of resources, intrinsic and/or extrinsic, that imbue individuals and/or groups who possess them with the ability to influence and/or determine another individual's or group's experiences, perceptions, attitudes, behaviors, and access to resources.

Privilege is a status, earned or assigned, that affords one power, earned and unearned.

Privileged Self is that part of the self that is connected to a social status or location imbued with power.

Relational Context acknowledges the self in relationship to other (SIRO).

Self of the Supervisor refers to the supervisor's conscious and unconscious values, attitudes, assumptions, biases, and behaviors based on his/her own race, ethnicity, culture, class, gender, religion, sexual orientation, family of origin, country of origin, age, and ability.

Self of the Therapist refers to the therapist's conscious and unconscious values, attitudes, assumptions, biases, and behaviors based on his/her own race, ethnicity, culture, class, gender, religion, sexual orientation, family of origin, country of origin, age, and ability.

Subjugated Self is that part of the self that is connected to a social status or location vulnerable to a more powerful social status or location.

Trauma Informed signifies a realization and understanding that oppressed, victimized and marginalized individuals and groups carry the traumatizing effects of such experiences and require support for healing and recovery.

HANDOUTS AND RESOURCES

Relational Ethics

> *We believe that fairness, trustworthiness, reciprocity between give and take, and equitability are the cornerstones for all healthy, functional, and viable relationships.*

Boszormenyi-Nagy and Spark (1984) coined the term *relational ethics* and used it to refer to dynamics and societal functioning that holds family relationships together through trustworthiness, reliability, and the principle of equitability. The ethics described here is concerned with achieving a balance of fairness among people, with reciprocity between give-and-take. This fairness and equitability is considered through a long-term family process, where the balance is preserved and all others take the interests of each into account. One person's interests are not the criterion for fairness, but rather the interests of each family member.

According to Nagy, each member is entitled to have his or her general interests and welfare considered by all other family members. While Nagy applied the principle of relational ethics largely to families and their members, we apply it more broadly as a governing principle for all human relationships.

REFERENCE

Boszormenyi-Nagy, I., & Spark, G. (1984). *Invisible Loyalties: Reciprocity in Intergenerational Family Therapy* (2nd ed.). New York, NY: Brunner/Mazel.

Sample Case Presentation Format Using a Multicultural Relational Perspective

Name: _____ **Date:** _____

1. Provide identifying information about your client:

    _____

2. State presenting issue in your client's own words:

    _____

3. Discuss significant contextual variables that may be connected to the presenting problem and/or your client's current circumstances:

    _____

4. Identify significant contextual variables that may impact the therapy relationship:

    _____

5. Attach cultural genogram of your client if appropriate.

    _____

6. Discuss how your client's story impacts you personally and emotionally:

    _____

7. State whether your client's personal story presents challenges and how your supervision might help you with these challenges:

    _____

8. Describe how you invite a conversation about similar and differing identities between yourself and your client and how you use yourself to facilitate this process:

    _____

9. Discuss how you explore the impact of power and privilege in your relationship with your client:

    _____

10. Identify what you particularly need from your supervisor and supervision group, if applicable, to facilitate your work with your client:

    _____

Note: "Client" refers to an individual, couple, or family seeking therapy.

Sample Framework for Establishing an Explicit Supervision Contract

1) Mechanics of Supervision

   - Logistics (date, time, compensation if relevant, etc.)
   - Changes (time, membership, format, etc.)—any and all changes that impact the supervisory relationship and/or process will be discussed and negotiated when unanticipated variables come into play
   - Supervisee Expectations and Responsibilities
   - Supervisor Expectations and Responsibilities
   - Format and Process of Evaluation

2) Making the Implicit Explicit

   - Theory of Change
   - Philosophy of Supervision
   - Bias Safeguards such as Management of Transference/Countertransference and Acknowledgment of Cultural Triggers
   - Deconstructing Power and Privilege in the Supervisory Relationship

3) Ethics

   - Professional Ethics—adhere to ethics of profession
   - Relational Ethics—how you value relationships in shared humanity

4) Critical issues that are highly relevant to culturally sensitive supervision should be discussed:

   - Therapist use of self(ves)
   - Supervisor use of self(ves)
   - Broker of Permission
   - Context Talk
   - Thinking Culturally/Contextually
   - Impact of Power
   - Impact of Privilege
   - Understanding of Trauma and Oppression
   - Self(ves) of the Therapist Considerations
   - Establishing an Effective Supervisory Relationship

Promoting Cultural Sensitivity Starter Kit

The promoting cultural sensitivity (PCS) starter kit provides the prospective supervisee with a thorough overview of the conceptual tools needed for the online supervision sessions. The PCS starter kit contains the following:

- MRP Core Beliefs and Values Handout

- Explanation of Multidimensional Self Handout

- Location of Self Handout

- Homework Policy Handout

- Cultural Genogram Handout

- Resources for More Information about Genograms

Once read, the supervisee should be prepared to discuss the contents of the Starter Kit with the supervisor and sign a Letter of Understanding and Consent, which may constitute the Supervisory Contract, unless otherwise indicated by the supervisor and/or the supervisee.

MRP CORE BELIEFS AND VALUES HANDOUT

The Multicultural Relational Perspective (MRP) is a worldview that provides an in-depth and comprehensive framework for clinical supervision. The MRP is a philosophical stance that is the conceptual foundation for this Manual. This approach is predicated on the premise that therapy and supervision are parallel processes and are organized around the following beliefs and values:

- The centrality of relationships and the notion that human suffering is located within relationships
- That cultural factors are salient contextual variables in our lives and must be attended to with humility, sensitivity, and competence
- That our understanding of socio-cultural trauma and the hidden wounds associated with it are essential to clinical effectiveness
- That an acute exploration of the self of the therapist and self of the supervisor issues are critical to the provision of effective therapy and supervision
- That clinicians explore and understand the role that their biases (unconscious and otherwise) may have on therapy and supervision

The following are additional core values associated with an approach to supervision centered on cultural sensitivity:

- Understanding one's self as a cultural being
- A focus on the self of the therapist/supervisor issues
- An examination of self in relationship to other
- Talking openly, honestly, and uninhibitedly about the varied dimensions of culture.
- Exploring and hypothesizing how presenting problems and the process of therapy may be informed, compounded, exacerbated, and/or ameliorated by one or more dimension(s) of culture
- Willingness to utilize self-disclosure and establishing comfort with it from all participants involved in the supervisory process, including the supervisor
- Participation in regular experiential exercises that may appear tangential but that are key to enhancing cultural awareness and sensitivity
- Provide access to raw clinical data via video streaming, audiotapes, or other technologies
- Agreement to a 9–12 month contract for supervision
- Understanding and attending to the dynamics of power, powerlessness, privilege, and subjugation

REFERENCE

Hardy, K., & Bobes, T. (2017) *Promoting Cultural Sensitivity in Supervision: A Manual for Practitioners.* New York, NY: Routledge.

EXPLANATION OF MULTIDIMENSIONAL SELF HANDOUT

Encourage the development of a Multidimensional View of the Self. The process of thinking culturally should ideally start with oneself (which is generally true for all principles associated with the MRP). Developing a multidimensional view of the self is the first crucial step towards beginning to see others more complexly, that is, culturally. Developing a deeper and more complex understanding of the self paves the way to understanding others similarly.

The development of a Multidimensional View of the Self challenges the notion that what is typically thought of as the self actually comprises many selves. For example, each of us has a gendered self, a racial self, a religious self, an ethnic self, a sexual orientation self, and Family of Origin (FOO) self as well as a host of others. Since many of our selves are socially constructed, they are imbued with varying degrees of power, powerlessness, privilege, and subjugation as they are reified in the larger culture. Many of us are equipped with both privileged and subjugated selves. As a Black, heterosexual, middle-class male, I possess several privileged selves: gender, sexual orientation, and class while also possessing a subjugated self, which is my racial self.

As each of us begins to see ourselves through the prism of our multiple selves including those that are privileged and subjugated, we are much better equipped to see others similarly. The more comprehensively we can see ourselves and others, the greater the degree of compassion, understanding, and humility we can have for each other (Hardy, 2016, p. 6).

REFERENCE

Hardy, K. V. (2016). Toward the Development of a Multicultural Relational Perspective in Training and Supervision. In K. V. Hardy & T. Bobes (Eds.), *Culturally Sensitive Supervision and Training: Diverse Perspectives and Practical Applications* (pp. 3–10). New York, NY: Routledge.

LOCATION OF SELF HANDOUT

An essential relational and executive skill for supervisors is to utilize the location of self-orientation, a fundamental component associated with opening the door to difficult dialogues (Watts Jones, 2010, 2016). Supervisors model identification of their social location by discussing how their cultural identities (i.e., gender, race, class, etc.) might influence therapy and supervision relationships. Location of self involves acknowledging our multiple selves and how we make them explicit.

Hardy (2016) further clarifies the Location or Use of Selves as an essential component of the MRP:

> The Location or Use of "Self" refers to the facility with which one can draw from the knowledge one has of one's self that can be accessed as a potential interpersonal resource to promote connections. The location or Use of "Self" is predicated on the effective use of "Self" disclosure which is an important component of an MRP.
>
> (Hardy, 2016, p. 6)

Supervisors who identify their social locations increase their capacities for cultural sensitivity and attunement to supervisees' lived experiences.

REFERENCES

Hardy, K. V. (2016). Toward the Development of a Multicultural Relational Perspective in Training and Supervision. In K. V. Hardy & T. Bobes (Eds.), *Culturally Sensitive Supervision and Training: Diverse Perspectives and Practical Applications* (pp. 3–10). New York, NY: Routledge.

Watts Jones, D. (2010). Location of Self: Opening the Door to Dialogue on Intersectionality in the Therapy Process. *Family Process, 49*(3), 405–420.

Watts Jones, D. (2016). Location of Self in Training and Supervision. In K. V. Hardy & T. Bobes (Eds.), *Culturally Sensitive Supervision and Training: Diverse Perspectives and Practical Applications* (pp. 16–24). New York, NY: Routledge.

HOMEWORK POLICY HANDOUT

Homework assignments are suggested at the end of each supervisory session and are intended to:

1. Encourage self-reflection
2. Connect one session to the next
3. Promote additional learning
4. Foster an element of intimacy in distance learning

Reflection papers are a valuable means of responding to homework assignments. Reflection papers are typically reviewed and discussed at the next supervision session unless otherwise negotiated between the supervisor and supervisee. The papers become an opportunity for the supervisor and supervisee to enrich and deepen the supervisory experience.

It is strongly recommended that homework assignments continue throughout the course of the online supervision. Responses to homework assignments may be submitted using available technologies.

CULTURAL GENOGRAM HANDOUT

THE CULTURAL GENOGRAM: AN APPLICATION

Kenneth V. Hardy, PhD & Tracey A. Laszloffy, PhD

This chapter originally appeared in The Reasonably Complete Systemic Supervisor Resource Guide *(Storm & Todd, 1997), which is out of print.*

How do I help my supervisees, especially non-minorities, talk about cultural issues in supervision and therapy? How important is it for supervisees to explore their cultural identities before they can deal effectively with cultural issues with their clients? And, how do I assist my supervisees in transferring the exploration of cultural issues in supervision to their work as therapists? Questions such as these are recurring queries for many supervisors as they struggle with finding concrete ways to facilitate the integration of cultural issues into clinical supervision.

The cultural genogram is a tool that you can use to explore culture in the context of supervision and ultimately therapy. The cultural genogram process promotes cultural awareness and sensitivity by helping supervisees to understand their cultural identities. Through this process supervisees gain greater insight into, and appreciation for, the ways in which culture impacts their personal and professional lives, as well as the lives of their clients. Due to limitations of space, we discuss the cultural genogram within the context of team supervision only.

The cultural genogram process is divided into three stages: 1) preparation and construction, 2) presentation and interpretation, and 3) synthesis. For a detailed discussion of the stages and steps of the cultural genogram process, the reader is referred to Hardy & Laszloffy (1995).

Stage One: Preparation and Construction

During this stage, supervisees are required/encouraged to research their culture-of-origin and prepare a cultural genogram that will be presented in supervision. A copy of "How to Prepare a Cultural Genogram" should be available to supervisees to help facilitate completion of this stage. This document outlines each step in stage one, and defines all essential terminology.

How to Prepare a Cultural Genogram

Culture-of-Origin: We define culture-of-origin as the group(s) from which an individual has descended over several generations.

Identify the groups that make up your culture-of-origin. Research each group you have identified as part of your culture-of-origin. Your research should culminate in the creation of a Cultural Framework Chart(s).

Cultural Framework Chart (CFC): A CFC comprises organizing principles, pride/ shame issues, and pride/shame symbols.

Create one chart for each group that comprises your culture-of-origin. Each chart should consist of the following:

- Organizing Principles: These are fundamental constructs which shape perceptions, beliefs, and behaviors of members of a group. These should be listed in the chart.

- Pride/Shame Issues: These originate and derive their meaning from organizing principles. They are aspects of a culture that are sanctioned as distinctly positive or negative. These should be listed on the chart.

- Symbols: These are used to visually depict each pride/shame issue. They should be placed directly on the chart beside each corresponding pride/shame issue.

Genogram: The genogram is a graphic depiction of one's family-of-origin. Through the use of colors and the placement of pride/shame symbols, the genogram reveals the cultural identities of each individual, as well as occurrence of specific pride/shame issues throughout the family system.

Construct at least a three generation genogram of your family-of-origin. The following should appear on the genogram:

- Colors: Select a color to represent each group in your culture-of-origin. Next, color-code the circles and squares on the genogram accordingly to depict the cultural identities of each individual.

- Pride/Shame Symbols: Place the symbols on the genogram to identify where various pride/shame issues are manifest.

Copyright © 1997 by Allyn and Bacon

Stage Two: Presentation and Interpretation

This stage involves the presentation of the cultural genogram. During the presentation, the supervisee begins by presenting the Cultural Framework Chart(s) (CFC) s/he has constructed for her/his culture-of-origin. Specifically, the supervisee briefly introduces and explains each of the organizing principles and pride/shame issues on her/his chart(s). When referring to each pride/shame issue, the supervisee should make corresponding references to the genogram as a way of demonstrating where each of the issues is manifest in her/his family. Thus the CFC(s) and the genogram are presented in a complementary and integrated manner.

Following the presentation, the supervisee should have the opportunity to respond to observations or questions that might have been generated for the supervisor and/or members of the supervision team. The purpose here is to identify significant culturally-based patterns, themes, or dynamics that might emerge for the supervisee, and for members of the supervision team as well.

It is helpful to have a designated facilitator during the actual presentation. Depending upon your theoretical orientation, you may prefer to assume the role of facilitator, assign it to another supervisee, or encourage the team to select one. Regardless of the methodology employed for selecting a facilitator, you are ultimately responsible for the supervision session. However, the individual(s) functioning as the facilitator actually directs the cultural genogram process.

The role of facilitator during the presentation process involves guiding the interaction between the presenting supervisee and the team. In this way, the facilitator remains "meta" to the process and helps to facilitate in a way that challenges and supports all members' exploration of their culturally-based beliefs, suppositions, and assumptions. In other words, this is not a linear process whereby only the presenting supervisee is challenged to think and learn about her/himself culturally. Rather, the process is intended to be interactive and systemic such that all members of the group are encouraged to identify and explore their culturally-based beliefs, suppositions, and assumptions.

The presenting supervisee, Alan, began by defining his culture-of-origin as German. He presented his CFC for German culture and explained each organizing principle. Next Alan described each German pride issue and referred to his genogram to demonstrate where each of these were manifest in his family system. However, with regard to German shame issues, Alan had drawn a picture of a grayish "blob" which he said depicted a generalized but unidentifiable kind of shame that's "just sort of all around but it can't be linked to anything in particular."

Members of the observing team asked Alan what his theory was about, why he was so adept at defining pride issues and yet was so inept at identifying shame issues? Alan suspected it was because he had not devoted enough time to preparing his genogram. However, one supervisee, Elana, explained to Alan that she believed the

Holocaust constituted a significant German shame issue, and as a Jew, she felt offended that he had failed to acknowledge this. Alan became sullen and said, "But what do you want me to do about that? I often feel like you want something from me but I don't know what. It makes it really hard for me to be around you." Elana answered by saying, "For starters what I want from you is for you to own the shameful parts of who you are. . . . I often feel this sense of anger toward you that I've never understood, but now I realize it's because I've always seen you as trying to show how perfect you are and you never own the ugly parts of yourself . . . and culturally-speaking, that really threatens me."

In this example, the cultural genogram process was a catalyst for promoting an exchange between two supervisees who were struggling with culturally-based issues. Alan, with regard to his German ancestry, was struggling with his shame, and Elana, in relation to her Jewish identity, was struggling with her fear and anger regarding the Holocaust. The cultural legacies of Germans and Jews in relation to the Holocaust linked and yet divided both individuals; although it had been between them for months, it had never been acknowledged. The facilitator used this interaction to help the two supervisees consider the implications their cultural legacies had in supervision and on their work as therapists.

The most critical dimension of this stage of the process involves helping supervisees make connections between their cultural legacies and identities, and their roles as members of the supervision team and as therapists. Thus, they should be encouraged to consider the ways in which their cultural selves shape how they interact in supervision and therapy.

Critical Tasks for Facilitators

There are several critical tasks for the facilitator to consider during the cultural genogram process. In situations where you assume the role of the facilitator, you therefore incur direct responsibility for attending to these tasks. When another member of the team assumes the role of the facilitator, you incur indirect responsibility for these tasks in the sense that you observe, and/or if deemed necessary, assist the facilitator.

First, it is important for you to be alert to helping supervisees distinguish between their family-of-origin and culture-of-origin. It is common for supervisees to blur the two, however, since the purpose of the exercise is to focus on cultural issues, it is important to keep family-of-origin and culture-of-origin clearly differentiated. Second, it is useful for you to attend to shame issues closely. Supervisees often struggle with identifying, and discussing shame issues because of the pain and discomfort this typically generates. Moreover, how supervisees respond to and communicate shame issues also may have cultural underpinnings. Relatedly, it is helpful for you to be sensitive to culturally-based reasons for the differences in how supervisees respond to and participate in the process. While differences may be attributable to family-of-origin variables, there also may be cultural explanations for particular differences.

It is further recommended that you manage your anxiety and reactivity. The degree to which you have explored your culturally-based pride/shame issues will enhance your ability to manage your anxiety and reactivity effectively with supervisees. Moreover, it is critical that you help supervisees to stay with the emotional intensity that often is generated during a cultural genogram presentation. Supervisors who have dealt with their cultural selves are better positioned to help supervisees work through their cultural issues.

Stage Three: Synthesis

In the third and final stage of the cultural genogram process, the presenting supervisee synthesizes what s/he has learned about her/himself culturally. Specific emphasis should be placed upon requiring the supervisee to explore the implications for their role as therapist. It is ultimately your responsibility to help supervisees make critical connections between what they discover during the cultural genogram process and therapy.

Summary

The preparation, presentation, and synthesis of a cultural genogram can be quite useful in helping supervisees and supervisors negotiate the cultural dimensions of supervision and ultimately therapy. When used effectively in supervision, the cultural genogram process can give direction to all those pragmatic, "how to" questions that often are asked regarding the integration and exploration of culture in supervision and therapy.

REFERENCES

Hardy, K. V., & Laszloffy, T. A. (1995). The Cultural Genogram: A Key to Training Culturally Competent Family Therapists. *Journal of Marital and Family Therapy, 21*, 227–237.

Storm, C. L., & Todd, T. C. (1997). *The Reasonably Complete Systemic Supervisor Resource Guide.* Needham Heights, MA: Allyn & Bacon.

Resources for More Information about Genograms

Hardy, K. V., & Laszloffy, T. A. (1995). The Cultural Genogram: Key to Training Culturally Competent Family Therapists. *Journal of Marital and Family Therapy, 21*(3), 227–237.

Hardy, K. V., & Laszloffy, T. A. (1997). The Cultural Genogram: An Application. In C. L. Storm & T. C. Todd (Eds.), *The Reasonably Complete Systemic Supervisor Resource Guide* (pp. 34–39). Needham Heights, MA: Allyn & Bacon.

McGoldrick, M. (2016). *The Genogram Casebook: A Clinical Companion to Genograms: Assessment and Intervention.* New York, NY: Norton.

McGoldrick, M., Gerson, R., & Petry, S. (2008). *Genograms: Assessment and Intervention* (3rd ed.). New York, NY: Norton.

Software for Creating and Editing Genograms

There are a number of computer applications available for developing genograms. One of these applications is called GenoPro (www.genopro.com). An Internet search using the keywords "cultural genogram software" will display a variety of other choices as well.

Professional Organizations

ADA National Network
Information, Guidelines, and Training on the Americans with Disabilities Act
(800) 949–4232
https://adata.org

American Association for Marriage and Family Therapy
112 South Alfred Street
Alexandria, VA 22314
(703) 838–9808
(703) 838–9805 (FAX)
www.aamft.org

American Counseling Association
6101 Stevenson Avenue
Alexandria, VA 22304
(703) 823–9800
(703) 823–0252 (FAX)
https://www.counseling.org

American Mental Health Counselors Association (AMHCA)
675 N. Washington, Suite 470
Alexandria, VA 22314
(703) 548–6002
www.amhca.org

American Psychiatric Association (APA)
1000 Wilson Boulevard, Suite 1825
Arlington, VA 22209–3901
(703) 907–7300
www.psych.org

American Psychological Association
750 First Street, NE
Washington, DC 20002–4242
(800) 374–2721 or (202) 336–5500
www.apa.org

California Association of Marriage and Family Therapists (CAMFT)
7901 Raytheon Road
San Diego, CA 92111–1606
(858) 292–2638
www.camft.org

Eikenberg Academy for Social Justice
Eikenberg Institute for Relationships
311 A West 50th Street
New York, NY 10019
(212) 956–2210
tier311@gmail.com

National Association of Social Workers
750 First Street, NE, Suite 800
Washington, DC 20002
(800) 742–4089
www.socialworkers.org

Index

n refers to note

acknowledgment 56
actions and reactions, concept 6
affect and cognition domain 5–6
Anderson, Tom 82
authenticity, in communication 56
awareness 4

Boszormenyi-Nagy, I. 135
Both/And thinking 3, 5, 48, 59
Boyd-Franklin, N. 13
broker of permission 3

challenge: and validation 16, 49; as invitation 52;
    avoiding questions 50; defined 7, 48; example of
    50, 59; *see also* VCR (validate, challenge,
    request) Approach
change 36
collaborative learning: about 75–76; live supervision
    80–82; reflecting teams 82–83; role-playing
    77–78; videotaping 79–80
communication 25, 56–57
competencies, of supervisors 3–4
congruency, in communication 56
contemplation 57
context 130
context map 10–12
Context Talk 55–59
contracts, for supervision: developing 32; fluidity of
    42; for online supervision 85–86; framework for
    42–43, 139
cultural framework charts (CFC) 66, 147, 148
cultural sensitivity: enhancing 37; facilitating,
    promoting 33; in online supervision 85–97;
    vs. cultural awareness 61–62; *see also*
    Promoting Cultural Sensitivity (PCS) Starter
    Kit
culture: and ethnicity 62, 64; diversity 3–4, 17–18,
    38, 39, 55; of origin 146–147, 148, 149;
    see also cultural framework charts (CFC);
    cultural sensitivity

deep listening 55–56
DeGruy Leary, J. 22
domains of interest 5–7, 7–8
Duffy, Sharon 43n

ecology, psychology, biology, concept 6
ethics 40, 43
ethnicity 62, 64, 93

facilitators: for genogram 68, 69, 148–150; for racial
    awareness exercise 107–113; for use of self
    exercise 100–103; supervisors as 15–16, 17
family orientation 130
family-of-origin (FOO): as social self 143; in
    genograms 63, 147; questioning issues of 87, 88;
    vs. culture-of-origin 149
feedback 56
functional/dysfunctional, concept 6

gender 37, 67, 88–89
genogram: as cultural tool 146; bias in 71–72;
    clinical implications of 70; example of 148–149;
    facilitator role 68, 69, 148–149; goal of 62;
    illustrated 63; in online supervision 89–90, 93;
    interpreting, presenting 66–69, 148–149;
    preparing 64–66, 67, 146–147; research
    implications of 70–71; software for 150;
    synthesis of 66, 68, 69, 150
growth, personal/professional 15

Hardy, K. V. 4, 7, 8–9, 22, 25–28, 144, 146
health/pathology, concept 6
homework policy handout 145

"I" messages 56
Integrated Developmental Model of supervision
    19n
intensity, in communication 56
intercultural marriage 65
intimacy, in communication 56

153

Lappin, J. 70
Laszloffy, T. A. 4, 7, 146
live supervision 80–82
location of self handout 144

meta-communication 56
microaggressive language 103–104, 104n
Multicultural Relational Perspective (MRP): about 4–5; and VCR approach 47; case presentation format 137; defined 130; developmental model for 15–19; handout for 142–143; key terms defined 130–131; outcomes survey 128–130; thinking contextually 7–8; thinking rationally 5–7
multiculturalism 131

"name it and claim it" 25, 26

one-way mirror 80–82
online supervision: check-in session for 92; considering culture in cases 96; engagement phase of 87; FOO questions 87–88; gender discussion 88–89; genogram presentation 89–90, 93; incorporating cultural sensitivity 85–86; potential of 85; pre-supervision phase 86–87; race, culture discussion 94–95; religion discussion 90–91; self of the therapist discussion 88–89; sexual orientation discussion 91–92; social class discussion 95–96; see also supervision; supervisors

past/present, concept 6
Pierce, C. M. 104n
Piercy, F. P. 43n
Post Traumatic Slavery Syndrome 22
power, defined 131
pride/shame issues 64–65, 147
privilege 131
privileged self 131
problems/solutions, concept 6
professional organizations 151–152
Promoting Cultural Sensitivity (PCS) Starter Kit 87, 141

race: and trauma 21–22; discussion on 23, 94–95; in use of self encounter 27; in VCR encounter 59; see also racial trauma; RASE (Racial Awareness Sensitivity Exercise)
racial trauma 21–23, 27
RASE (Racial Awareness Sensitivity Exercise): exercise summary 114; facilitator role, guidelines 111–113; purpose of 106; questions for 107–109; sample processing questions 113–114; settings, format for 109–111

reflection 57
relational ethics 135
religion 90–91
request: connecting 50; defined 48; example of 59; using multisystems levels 3, 13; see also VCR (validate, challenge, request) Approach
role-playing 77–78

Self and Other domain 7
self of the supervisor 131
self of the therapist 85, 86, 88, 131
self-knowledge 57
self-orientation 8–9
sensitivity 4
sexual orientation 91–92
silence, in conversation 57
social class 95–96
Spark, G. 135
Sprenkle, D. H. 43n
Steiny, Nancy 43n
subjugated self 131
subjugation 22
SuperVision 5
supervision: addressing literature on 41; addressing microaggressive language 103–104; articulating philosophy for 99–100; culturally informed questions 18; developing, framing 5–6; difficult dialogues 105; evaluations of process 123–125; identifying subjugated, privileged selves 102–103; mechanics of 42; models for 34; MRP in 4–5; parallel with therapy 4; philosophy for 31–32; power, responsibility in 51; questions as interventions 16–17; relating to therapy 35; satisfaction based on MRP training 125–126; sharing cultural experience 101–102; use of self exercise 100–101; see also online supervision
supervisors: becoming 83; core competencies of 3–4; cultural tasks of 15–16; evaluation of qualities, skills 126–128; expectations of 76; self-assessment tools for 119–122; using multisystems levels 13; see also online supervision
symbols, colors, in genogram 65, 147

tasks of the privileged 57–58
tasks of the subjugated 58
"The View from Black America: Listening to the Untold Stories": 26–27
therapeutic response 57
therapists: and cultural genograms 70; as activist 26–28; cultural competency for 4; supervision of 9, 13; using multisystems levels 13; using personal experience 26–28

therapy 4, 51
"Thinking Contextually", concept 7–8
"Thinking Rationally", concept 5–6
transparency, in communication 56
trauma, racial 22–27
trauma informed 131

validate/challenge domain 7
validation: authenticity in 52; avoiding aggression 51; defined 47–48; degrees of 49; intimacy in 52; preceding challenge 48; recipient cues for 49

VCR (validate, challenge, request) Approach: about 47–48; confusing stages of 51; expansion in 49; interrelating 50; principles of 48–49; sequencing steps of 52–53; skills needed for 59; terminology for 50–51; using 3, 16, 18
verbal, nonverbal communication, concept 6–7
videotaping 79–80
vignettes 9, 13, 105–106, 112–113; multilayered realities in supervision 13

Whites 22–23

#0115 - 210918 - C0 - 279/216/9 - PB - 9780415787680